ROUTLEDGE LIBRARY EDITIONS: ISLAMIC THOUGHT IN THE MIDDLE AGES

Volume 3

IBN RUSHD (AVERROES)

IBN RUSHD (AVERROES)

DOMINIQUE URVOY

Translated by
OLIVIA STEWART

LONDON AND NEW YORK

First published in 1991 by Routledge

This edition first published in 2016
by Routledge
2 Park Square, Milton Park, Abingdon, Oxon OX14 4RN

and by Routledge
711 Third Avenue, New York, NY 10017

Routledge is an imprint of the Taylor & Francis Group, an informa business

© 1991 Dominique Urvoy

All rights reserved. No part of this book may be reprinted or reproduced or utilised in any form or by any electronic, mechanical, or other means, now known or hereafter invented, including photocopying and recording, or in any information storage or retrieval system, without permission in writing from the publishers.

Trademark notice: Product or corporate names may be trademarks or registered trademarks, and are used only for identification and explanation without intent to infringe.

British Library Cataloguing in Publication Data
A catalogue record for this book is available from the British Library

ISBN: 978-1-138-93913-4 (Set)
ISBN: 978-1-315-66645-7 (Set) (ebk)
ISBN: 978-1-138-94250-9 (Volume 3) (hbk)
ISBN: 978-1-138-94738-2 (Volume 3) (pbk)

Publisher's Note
The publisher has gone to great lengths to ensure the quality of this reprint but points out that some imperfections in the original copies may be apparent.

Disclaimer
The publisher has made every effort to trace copyright holders and would welcome correspondence from those they have been unable to trace.

IBN RUSHD (AVERROES)

Dominique Urvoy

Translated by Olivia Stewart

London and New York

First published 1991
by Routledge
11 New Fetter Lane, London EC4P 4EE

Simultaneously published in the USA and Canada
by Routledge
a division of Routledge, Chapman and Hall, Inc.
29 West 35th Street, New York, NY 10001

© 1991 Dominique Urvoy

Printed in Great Britain by Clays Ltd, St Ives plc

All rights reserved. No part of this book may be reprinted or
reproduced or utilized in any form or by any electronic,
mechanical, or other means, now known or hereafter invented,
including photocopying and recording, or in any information
storage or retrieval system, without permission in writing from
the publishers.

British Library Cataloguing in Publication Data
Urvoy, Dominique
Ibn Rushd (Averroes). – (Arabic thought and culture)
1. Arab philosophy. Averroes, 1126–1198
I. Title   II. Series
181.9

Library of Congress Cataloging in Publication Data
Urvoy, Dominique.
Ibn Rushd (Averroes)/ Dominique Urvoy; translated by Olivia
Stewart.
p.   cm. – (Arabic thought and culture)
Includes bibliographical references (p.   ).
1. Averroes, 1126–1198.   2. Philosophy, Medieval.   I. Title.
II. Series.
B749.Z7U78   1990
181'.9–dc20   90–8426

ISBN 0 415 02141 3
ISBN 0 415 05567 9 (pbk.)

CONTENTS

INTRODUCTION	1
Historical and cultural context	3
Biography and family background	29
1 THE MAJOR OPTIONS	39
The scientific options	41
Methodological consequences	55
Cultural complements	59
Involvement in the Muslim community	64
2 THE INTERPRETATION OF ALMOHADISM	69
Rushdian theology	71
The philosophical implications	81
3 A 'HUMAN' KNOWLEDGE	90
Reasoning	92
The status of the intellect	99
The human community and the political community	109
4 AN AMBIGUOUS AUDIENCE	116
The Muslim milieu	116
The Jewish milieu	122
The medieval Christian orientalists	127
NOTES	132
BIBLIOGRAPHICAL GUIDE	134
History of Rushdian studies	134
Historical sources	137
Texts	139
Occidental Arab writers	139
Ibn Rushd	140
The current state of the questions	145
Index	149

IBN RUSHD (AVERROES)

The twelfth-century philosopher Ibn Rushd, also known as Averroes, is one of the most important philosophers of the Arab Middle Ages. He played a crucial role in the transmission of classical philosophy to Islam, and his work had a profound influence on western scholasticism and on aspects of Renaissance thought.

Going well beyond the Eurocentrist view which sees Ibn Rushd as little more than an intermediary between Aristotle and the scholastics, this book explores the main elements of his thought against the historical and cultural background of Muslim Spain. Dominique Urvoy gives a full account of Ibn Rushd's most important works, including his scientific, medical and legal as well as philosophical writings. He shows that Ibn Rushd's work formed part of the wider movement of Almohadism, a politico-religious reform movement which had a great intellectual impact in Muslim Spain. Ibn Rushd was regarded by many as a propagandist, and the book seeks to understand the ambiguous reception of his thought. It traces the rise and fall of his reputation, and attempts to explain how a major figure can suffer prolonged eclipses of popularity.

Dominique Urvoy is Professor of Arabic Studies at the University of Toulouse-le Mirail. The book has been translated from the original French manuscript by Olivia Stewart.

INTRODUCTION

Why should we read a twelfth-century writer known primarily as a 'commentator' of Aristotle? Might there be a reason other than pure academic interest — whether this be focused upon the figure of Ibn Rushd who stands out in the history of the Arab world for his appropriation of the classical heritage, or upon the writer Averroes who had such a profound influence on Western scholasticism, its subsequent questioning, and finally on aspects of the Renaissance itself?

In 1976, on the celebration of the 850th anniversary of Ibn Rushd's birth, R. Arnaldez drew attention both to the 'historical' nature of his work, packed as it is with obsolete problems, and to the value of setting it in its Muslim context in the light, *inter alia*, of juridical thought and its methodology. He pointed too to the dangers of seeking questions in Ibn Rushd's writings which the author could never have asked.

Renan's pioneering work of 1861, admirable for its time, suffers from his indirect acquaintance with Ibn Rushd's work which he studied through Latin or Hebrew translations. More serious though is its tendency — despite the care of the researcher — to view the Muslim author as a free thinker along nineteenth-century lines or to regard him as a forerunner of the 'subjective immortality' of Auguste Comte via his theory on the unity of the Agent Intellect.

Similarly, there are a number of Muslims who as a result of the current tensions within their culture tend to advocate the simple resurrection of *Falsafa* as a rational attitude justified and even implied within the revelation of the Koran. However, in failing to situate Ibn Rushd's work in the context of the rationalizing reform of the Almohads, they rob it of its essence, reducing it to a collection of slogans which at their most extreme are quite as obscurantist as those of their fundamentalist opponents. In the past the Paduan Averroism of the Renaissance also fell into this trap.

This brief introduction to the study of Ibn Rushd's work aims to present a thinker working within a given context and asking questions arising within this context but, as with all true philosophy, taking them to their ultimate limits. To lock the writer within a historical or sociological determinism would be to lapse into empty erudition, and the specific aim of replacing Ibn Rushd in his context must be to depict the roots of a thought which was to develop beyond the seeds from which it first sprang. It is in this dialectical interplay between the contemporary issue and the foreshadowing of the universal that I believe philosophical work can be carried out. Perhaps too this approach represents a means of reconciling our historical vision with the Rushdian conception of a *Philosophia perennis* perpetually enacted in one or other part of the world.

It also helps avoid certain errors in the historical appreciation of the work. First, it helps get away from the Eurocentrist view which sees Ibn Rushd as little more than an intermediary between Aristotle and the scholastics. This study aims to restore the historical aspects of his work to their true importance, concentrating on their most prominent elements rather than conducting a detailed examination of his analyses. The purpose of this is to discover a specific mindset fitting within a particular historical situation. This situation and this mindset are laden with questions on which the present work aims to shed light.

Moreover, this approach enables us to challenge certain over-hasty criticisms arising out of a schematic vision of history. In particular, H. Corbin has emphasised Ibn Rushd's lack of subsequent influence on the Muslim world and he compares this to the impact of Eastern thinkers, especially Avicenna and Suhrawardi. He sees this as a penalty of Ibn Rushd's failure to appreciate the prophetic impact of Arab thought – something which, by symbolic contrast, was understood by his compatriot and near contemporary Ibn Arabi who was to 'conquer' the East. It is strange here to see such a belligerent opponent of historicism make use of such an excessively historicist argument.

As we shall see, Ibn Rushd's work formed part of the wider movement of Almohadism, and his audience dwindled as the movement itself suffered reversals, first as a result of the reaction in al-Andalus associated with Maliki traditionalism, and later with

INTRODUCTION

the rapid disappearance of the Muslim Spanish heartlands in the face of the Reconquista. The downfall of Ibn Rushd should not be regarded as an inherently justified verdict of history, any more than this was the case, for example, regarding the 'martyr' of the gnostic movement of Alamut. Both cases involved the intervention of external events which can be seen as a separate factor that neither validates nor invalidates the thought concerned.

* * *

With a view to reducing typographical problems in a study intended for a general readership, transcriptions of the emphatic Arabic letters (stressed d,s,t,z) will not be given. Other letters to be noted are:

kh = German ch
dh = spirant interdental
'- = sounded laryngeal spirant (for *ayn*) or
     vocalic striking up (for *hamza*)
gh = guttural r, sounded velar spirant

Also in order to simplify presentation, only those references not included in the bibliography will be noted in the text. Otherwise the work to which reference is made will be indicated in shortened form within the text so that the reader can, if desired, refer to the bibliography for the complete title.

HISTORICAL AND CULTURAL CONTEXT

The Muslims of al-Andalus liked to believe that the peninsula was empty of thought before the introduction of their own civilization. While it is true that both Seneca and his nephew, the philosopher-poet Lucan, were born in Cordoba, it was in Rome that both received their education and produced their works. In the Visigothic period, Saint Isidore, a seventh-century Bishop of Seville and later Braulio of Saragossa only preserved remnants of classical learning. Hence the historian Sa'id of Toledo stated that:

In early times Spain was devoid of science. None of its inhabitants achieved fame in this field. One can only point in a few places to the ancient monuments erected by the Roman kings (. . . .). This state of affairs persisted until the Muslims settled there.

(*Tabaqat al-umam*, ed. Cheikho, al-Machriq, Oct. 1911, p.666)

This highly biased view led them to ignore important phenomena such as the interesting attempt at christological thought represented by the Adoptionism of Elipandus, Archbishop of Toledo in the eighth century. The great religious historian Ibn Hazm, who was familiar with the Christian controversies of the East, completely ignored this Spanish contribution and also its continuation in his own milieu in the movement aiming to assimilate certain aspects of Nestorian thought.[1]

It is quite possible that there was a certain degree of affectation in this ignorance, since some curious similarities have been noted between the work of Muslim scholars and the Spanish Christian tradition. For example, Ibn Hazm created philosophical divisions which he recognised as completely different from those of Eastern Islam and which S. Gomez Nogales has found to be a replica of those of Saint Isidore of Seville.

On the other hand, in their desire to stress the beneficial influence of Islam, both Ibn Hazm and Sa'id highlighted the work of the ascetic Ibn Masarra of Cordoba (269/883–319/931) picking out every minor speculative element in a way that later led the Spanish Arabist Asin Palacios considerably to overestimate the work.[2] While not lacking in coherence, this work contains very little in the way of speculation and can in no way be considered a reflection of Eastern thought (Mu'tazilism – the first school of Muslim theology, and Batinism – esoteric doctrines).

Of far greater significance is that its development follows the same patterns as another gnostic movement indigenous to Spain, i.e. the Pricillianism of the fourth century. Both were primarily ascetic movements which, as such, opposed the clergy or ulema accusing them of compromise with the outside world. Their doctrines were little more than a justification elaborated *a posteriori*. These included claims to prophetic charisma rendering the movement independent of the church or the Traditions, segregation from the world and by extension the right to lie when the truth must be concealed. They also sanctioned a certain degree of reference to the works of the *Apocrypha* or to a tradition tracing

INTRODUCTION

back beyond the Prophet to ancient sources of wisdom, with allegorical interpretation serving to reconcile the two.

Thus Ibn Hazm, recognizing that the Andalusian thinkers had little interest in *Kalam* (apologetic theology) hoped through a sort of exaggeration to find in Ibn Masarra a spokesman of Eastern thought in Spain, whereas he was a representative of a variety of *shu'ubiya* or claim of the converted peoples.

In the fifth/eleventh century Ibn Hazm's thought was highly original, but unique and completely isolated. It constituted a major effort to reconsider the whole problem of Revelation, with its implications for the theory of language, working from a perspective rooted in Andalusian politics. It is this perspective, i.e. the author's loyalty to the defunct Ummayad dynasty and opposition to the dispersion of power under the taifa kings, which formed the key to his thinking, and its development was consistently shaped by this basic stance.

The first true 'philosophical system' to be developed in al-Andalus did not appear until the time of the Jewish thinker Ibn Gabirol (c. 1020–1057). His thought developed in the unique environment of Saragossa which had a thriving Jewish community in contact with Kairwan from which it inherited a scholastic neoplatonism that formed an integral part of the culture. The city also had a group of independent Muslims, some of whom helped in the diffusion of the oriental encyclopedia of the Brothers of Purity which reached them from the East. Added to this, the proximity of the Christian countries maintained an intellectual ferment which was to lead to the major translating activity of al-Andalus in the twelfth century. These factors also explain the non-confessional character of the philosophical part of Ibn Gabirol's work.

It is, however, only with him that the history of Andalusian thought starts to develop coherence. Hence it is possible to distinguish a sort of dialectic between the systems, which move from neoplatonism to the Aristotelianism of al-Farabi, and then to a more mystical perspective starting with Ibn Sina (Avicenna). The Jews played an important part in the first and third of these stages, while it was exclusively Muslims who instigated the second.

Little is known of the origins of *Falsafa* (philosophy of Hellenic inspiration) in the Muslim West. From the reign of al-Hakam II (third quarter of the fourth/tenth century) works of philosophy had been introduced into al-Andalus, and a whole group of scholars

5

had set to work studying them. Some were Christians, like the Bishop Recemundo and his pupil the Bishop Abu-l-Harith, some Jews, and others Muslims of Christian descent such as Maymun (Marcus) or of Jewish descent such as, later, the astronomer Abu Ja'afar Yusuf b. Hasday. Mainly though they were of original Muslim stock, and the oldest had themselves studied in the East.

This group included few philosophers by training. The majority were men of letters who were particularly concerned with the opposition between Greek logic and Arabic grammar. It was this movement that produced the first treatises of introduction to philosophy which were to pave the way for Ibn Hazm's (universally condemned) attempt to re-elaborate Aristotelian logic using terms from contemporary life and Muslim law.

Ibn Gabirol was a forerunner, but because of his marginal position was destined not to have any great influence in Muslim circles. The real initiator of Andalusian *Falsafa* was Malik b. Wuhayb of Seville (453/1061–524/1130) who was dubbed 'the philosopher of the West' for his explanations of the works of Aristotle and al-Farabi. Why he deserved this reputation is not clear since he left only one treatise on the principles of logic which has now been lost. However, he did support the younger scholar Ibn Bajja (d.533/1138) who was also educated in the unique environment of his native Saragossa.

Ibn Bajja (Avempace) is a seminal figure in the Muslim thought of the West. Though unfinished, his work was to be a major influence on both Ibn Rushd and the Scholastics in the field of philosophy, and in the field of science on the work of Albertus Magnus. However, it also represents a crucial juncture in the formation of a 'philosophical milieu' in al-Andalus, and with it the intellectual isolation described above was finally broken.

His work combines two elements for the first time. First, it contains a new and fertile problematic of the kind not found in thinkers such as Ibn Masarra or neoplatonists such as Ibn al-Sid of Badajoz (444/1052–521/1127). Second, it takes a precise stance in relation to the current position of philosophical thought in the Arabo-Muslim world as a whole, whereas Ibn Hazm and Ibn Gabirol despite the richness of their perspectives were far more a-temporal in approach.

It is generally accepted that *Falsafa*, which was established in the time of al-Kindi (c.185/796–260/873) assumed its true character with al-Farabi (259/872–339/950) who united the logical

INTRODUCTION

discipline and physics of Aristotle to an emanatist schema of the world. This very specific fusion was completed by Ibn Sina (370/ 980–428/1037) who placed greater emphasis on the religious aspect of this approach extending it to an intellectualist mysticism. This veritable 'culture' was, with the exception of logic, entirely rejected by the great theologian of Sunni Islam Abu Hamid al-Ghazali (450/1059–501/1111). Ghazali did not attempt to propose an alternative system but concentrated on destroying the claims of *Falsafa* by demonstrating its contradictions (*Tahafut al-falasifa*). He did this in order to force a return to a fideist attitude in the overall conception of the world, and to a mystical doctrine of delight (*dhawq*) on the level of practice.

These dates clearly indicate the time gap between East and West in the field of *Falsafa*. In the West it arose not only after an evolution but also after a crisis. A disciple and friend of Ibn Bajja, Ibn al-Imam, who spent the last part of his life in the East, haughtily declared that it was not until the arrival of Ibn Wuhayb and above all his own master that Spain really grasped the heritage of the Ancient World. By this he was referring to the rupture that took place then with the old intellectualism, which was based on the naive conviction that correct reasoning could lead only to true religion.

Ibn Bajja, however, did confront al-Ghazali's critique of reason. He did not formulate a direct refutation (this was left to Ibn Rushd), but instead claimed to transcend his critique. While adopting the objective of ultimate happiness pursued by the mystics, Ibn Bajja did not accept that happiness lies in delight. In his view it was achieved through science, of which pleasure was not the objective but merely an accident never pursued for its own sake. He accused al-Ghazali of replacing the rational faculty with one governed by the appetites. Ibn Bajja in fact presented a somewhat caricatural version of his adversary's position, interpreting the mystics' notion of 'union' simply as the union of the three faculties of apprehension — common sense, imagination and memory. This enabled him to draw an opposition between pure knowledge and semblances of the truth, between pure spiritual forms which alone can lead to knowledge and the individual spiritual form with which the mystic must be content.

Ibn Bajja thus claimed to overcome al-Ghazali's critique by formulating a unified theory of knowledge. Going further even than Aristotle, he pushed the definition of the status of the intellect (*oql*) to its limits in his *Treatise on the union of the (agent) intellect with man (acquired intellect)* which completes the description of the philosopher's approach given in *The Regime of the Solitary*.

According to Ibn Bajja there are substances that have no relation to matter and which the human intellect is capable of perceiving. This direct knowledge of the beyond enables union with the Agent Intellect from below and represents the ultimate perfection of the human intellect. Natural perfection is constituted by acquisition of the faculties that relate to determinate objects, and is therefore a corruptible form of perfection, whereas union of the acquired intellect with the Agent Intellect is a divine form of perfection transcending individuals. From this is drawn his declaration of the unity of the human intellect.

In his great debate with Ghazali Ibn Rushd simply reiterated this whole theory. However, his work was not simply a continuation or completion of Ibn Bajja's, which had been interrupted possibly under tragic circumstances. Whereas Ibn Bajja viewed the philosopher as a 'solitary' figure, Ibn Rushd's work aimed to provide instruction – certainly not of a kind accessible to the masses, but nevertheless directed towards the body of the elite.

This change of attitude was due to another factor totally independent of the first – i.e. the politico-religious reform introduced by the Almohads. This movement of Moroccan Berber origin had antecedents and driving factors specific to the Maghreb. However, its intellectual impact in al-Andalus cannot be properly appreciated without looking at it in relation to a tendency that took shape in that country, and against which Ibn Bajja's individual reaction was specifically directed. This tendency might be described as 'the Ghazalian temptation'.

Ibn Hazm was the only Andalusian thinker who could claim a grasp of the entire field of Muslim intellectual life. His thought extended not only to speculative questions and questions of individual practice, but encompassed the entire subject of the reception of religious revelation as well as *fiqh* (Law). This thought centred round a literalist approach and consisted in an exclusivity that was a curious mixture of great historical erudition and complete contempt for specific modifications brought about by history. Hence, the synthesis of the Eastern thinker, al-Ghazali, was far more attractive to the Muslims of Spain. Rejecting outright only some very extreme theories of Greek or Persian origin which

INTRODUCTION

had barely touched al-Andalus, he accepted the validity of theological apologetics (*Kalam*), of logic, and even of neoplatonist arguments. In the notion of 'revival of the Religious sciences' his approach preserved both collective history and the inner life, politics and mysticism.

The attraction of this outlook extended even to the Jewish community. Yehuda ha-Levi, famous singer of the return to Zion, borrowed a great deal from Ghazali's critique of philosophy in his attempt to revitalize his own religion. Also the mystic Bahya b. Paquda, abandoning to a certain extent the tradition of his people, drew on ancient Muslim mysticism via a source common to Ghazali and himself.

Amongst the Muslims, Ghazali's influence made itself felt in various ways. One of his followers was the Grand Qadi of Seville Abu Bakr b. al-'Arabi (468/1076–543/1148) who remained very close to his hierarchical syncretism. He was also the principal spiritual authority in the time of the Almoravid dynasty, who at the end of the fifth/eleventh century and beginning of the seventh/ thirteenth century wanted to bolster Muslim authority in the face of the Christians in the north of the peninsula, and also to strengthen the personal faith of the believers by implementing a return to rigorous discipline.

Another of his disciples, Ibn Husayn of Toledo, re-introduced the teaching of Ghazali in the continuation of ancient ascetic Andalusian schools in which renunciation (*zuhd*) served to counterbalance the legalism of *fiqh*. On the other hand, in the work of Abd al-Rahman al-Labasi, whose activities were divided between Guadix, Granada and Malaga, the Ghazalian influence is clearly drawn from the Sufi aspects. Subsequently this influence was to become increasingly diverse and was complicated by external and even contradictory additions.

It was in this milieu that a famous episode took place, and one which has frequently been misinterpreted, i.e. the official burning of al-Ghazali's works which were defended only by the religious men of Almeria. These events have been interpreted on the one side as a refusal by the Almoravid jurists to accept the greatest attempt undertaken within Islam to unite its mystical heritage with *fiqh*, and on the other as a resistance characteristic of a town which was to become one of the main centres of mysticism in the peninsula.

However, this interpretation does not hold if we distance

9

ourselves from the accounts of the chroniclers, which explicitly or implicitly prejudge the events, and undertake instead a simple statistical examination of the tendencies current at the time (see Urvoy, *Le Monde des ulemas andalous*, pp.129–31). There were at least two movements native to al-Andalus which attempted to combine mysticism and *fiqh*. The first was founded in the fifth/eleventh century by Ibn Abi Zamanin and grew into a brotherhood which united some of the most important figures of the age. The other movement, which arose later, was limited to the figure of al-Turtushi who, despite being based in Alexandria, had many followers in al-Andalus. Turtushi accused Ghazali of having poorly assimilated the teachings of Sufism and for his part expressed a preference for the old tradition of renunciation.

At the beginning of the sixth/twelfth century, with the exception of a few individuals who exploited Sufism for political ends and were treated as rebels, those who claimed allegiance not just to the teachings of Ghazali but to the man himself constituted a very small fringe. This group was not fully aligned with either the legalist camp – who formed the majority in al-Andalus – nor with the minority movement aspiring to religious revival which was respected by the authorities as long as it remained loyal. The Almoravid campaign against Ghazali was directed not against those who took up a definite position, but against the advocates of syncretism.

This impression is reinforced by a document issued directly from the Almoravid chancellory dating from a later stage when the dynasty was beginning to crumble in Morocco under the pressure of the Almohad movement. In a letter from the emir to the qadis of Valencia, dated 538/1143 (at which point Ibn Rushd was seven years old), the ruler made no mention of the doctrines of his new Maghrebi opponents who as yet had no following in the peninsula. Instead he drew attention to the threats of heresy internal to al-Andalus and which might be a source of trouble.

The fact that the letter concerns the region of Valencia, a bastion of tradition, excludes the possibility that the letter was referring to Sufism as such. The reference is simply to heretical books in general, 'especially those of Abu-Hamid al-Ghazali'.[3] These were to be tracked down and burned in their entirety. Investigations were to be made and an oath extracted from whoever was suspected of harbouring them.

This condemnation was not only the product of juridical

INTRODUCTION

sectarianism. The letter opens with a triple statement of intent of a typically moralizing nature: prayer is the best path to salvation; holy war is not only the duty of the community but of each individual and is an essential part of the faith; justice and equity must be upheld especially by those of high rank.

This profession of faith reveals how the dynasty was haunted by fear of the disintegration of al-Andalus in the face of the Christian offensive. In its desire to avoid compromise and equivocation it strove to restore to each citizen a sense of their responsibilities as a Muslim. It was destined to fail in this and, as we shall see, so too were the Almohads. Syncretism and retreat into the imagination were to triumph in al-Andalus resulting in the loss of the country for Islam.

Cordoba was in the forefront of resistance to this syncretizing movement. The man responsible for its initial condemnation was the Grand Qadi of Cordoba, Ibn Hamdin (439/1047–508/1114), described by Ibn 'Atiya as 'an outstanding man of science, intransigent concerning the truth and exercising a beneficial influence'. He set down the grounds for his condemnation in a written *Refutation* (*radd*) which has now been lost.

Although this may appear to have had little impact outside his own circle of followers, in fact it marked the beginning of a whole series of refutations of which the main passages were soon gathered together by Muhammad al-Ilbiri (458/1064-5–537/1142-3) in his *Accounts and texts concerning the destruction of Ghazali*.[4] Al-Ilbiri was not a jurist of narrow outlook but employed the methodology of his discipline (*usul al-fiqh*) together with apologetic theology, and also had a knowledge of mysticism in which he produced a synopsis of an important ancient text.

This provides confirmation that it was not so much the disciplines embraced by the work of Ghazali that came under attack, but the syncretism itself. While this was ultimately destined to triumph, the opposing viewpoint nevertheless left marks which can be traced up until the eighth/fourteenth century in the Kingdom of Granada.

The Almohad reforms were another aspect of the struggle against syncretism. The founder of the Almohad movement was the Berber Ibn Tumart (c.471–4/1078–81–524/1130). He began studying in a milieu Islamized some time before by the Kharijis, and the basic elements of this conception of the religion visibly shaped his own doctrine. This is evident in his insistence upon divine 'promise

11

and threats' which serve as a link between human activities and revelation, as well as in the reduction of the attributes of God to simple designations, and in the concept of the internal necessity of divine action.

Moreover, according to some Eastern writers, Ibn Tumart would have been a pupil in Cordoba of the qadi Ibn Hamdin who headed the opposition to Ghazali. At the time when the Almoravid dynasty was establishing itself in Spain he doubtless judged the opportunities for study there to be inadequate and left for the East where he studied mostly in Iraq. None of the Eastern masters attributed to him enable us – with our present knowledge – to explain the structure of the doctrine he went on to elaborate. This doctrine provided a basis first for the movement of reform, and later for the establishment of the empire he was to launch on his return to the Maghreb.

The doctrine has two apparently opposing aspects: a rational profession of faith, and a wholly positive juridical doctrine. The opposition of the two is made evident by the nature of the former. However, because of its historical importance we shall start by looking at the latter. In its practical aspects this doctrine constituted a juridical reform which followed on from that of the early Almoravids. This is clear in its scrupulous respect for legal provisions – a respect which extended into the field of law the activities of moral censorship undertaken by Ibn Tumart on his return to his country. He recalls that the bandit must be put to death and the thief have his hand cut off, but if they have already undergone another punishment such as whipping no further action can be taken. The penalties of mutilation not prescribed, but which the rulers tended to use liberally, were similarly condemned.

All this seems to take us a long way from philosophy. However, these issues which were of much greater interest to the masses than lofty speculations, are by no means devoid of intellectual significance. Unlike the Almoravids Ibn Tumart did not look to the ancient authorities to set the norms, but to the Revelation itself. Or rather – doubtless mistakenly from a historical point of view – he attributed these excessive punishments to a disregard for general rules in favour of the consideration of individual cases and immediate interests. In the case of the Maliki Almoravids this same legalistic approach led to the resurgence of an entire literature dealing with individual cases (*furu'*) – though tempered by

INTRODUCTION

methodological elaboration which took into account the debate between their own juridical school and the Shafi'is. In this instance, however, it led to a return to the very source of the Law.

Contemporary observers were particularly struck by this aspect, describing the Almohad doctrine as 'the doctrine of thought' (*madhhab al-fikr*). In fact it was an attempt to avoid the arbitrary which, however, did not go as far as the literalism of Ibn Hazm and which took historical necessities into consideration. The Almohad doctrine rejected Ibn Hazm's idea that there is always and in all cases a 'text' which can serve as a 'basis'. Instead it sided with the Shafi'i school which stated that reasoning by analogy – applying a specific passage of the Revelation to a certain situation for which it had not made provision – can provide a solution. While this was undoubtedly weaker than material drawn from the tradition itself, it was nevertheless admissible when no tradition existed for the subject in question.

Thus, least rigorous of the schools was ancient Malikism in which consideration of circumstances played a major part and which considered reference to the Medinite tradition an adequate basis for certainty. Higher up the scale stood the Shafi'i school of which Ibn Hazm was initially a member before he broke away to adopt a literalistic approach. This was the school of Ghazali, and some Eastern writers suggested that Ibn Tumart was also amongst its followers. Its doctrine claims simply to draw out the conclusions from the final premise of Malikism in elaborating a Methodology of Law. The Maliki school in its turn underwent a certain reform. Ibn Hazm's main opponent, al-Baji, did not accept certain laxities in the Shafi'i doctrine, for example the use of analogical reasoning based on a simple resemblance between the objects of consideration.

Ibn Tumart for his part also accepted that Islam was first and foremost a practical system, and that it was better to risk error by acting on personal judgement than to abstain completely. However, he maintained that analogy could not be invoked except between things falling into perfectly identical juridical categories, or in the case of a specific law when it was based on terms similarly employed.

Hence when definite proof was lacking, not only analogy but opinion could play a role in determining practice – be it individual reasoning (*ra'y*) applied to general questions or a judgement of probability (*zann*) in interpretation of the Revelation. On the other hand, Ibn Tumart refused to consider these solutions as absolute, thus by slavish imitation (*taqlid*) endowing with the necessity of reason the passions of one individual who was considered an authority. Individual reasoning was of no use in *establishing* laws. The role attributed to the necessity of reason when it was brought to bear upon pure ideas will be discussed in due course. In dealing with empirical matters it could only provide a possible answer open to a degree of doubt. The truth could only be approached through the mutual correction of scholars over the ages.

Personal effort (*ijtihad*) could only be applied to the Revelation. Its laws, established according to methods whose varying degrees of certainty were discussed at length by Ibn Tumart, did not have the necessity of reason but that, no less strong, which was conferred upon them by divine authority. Al-Shafi'i's distinction between knowledge which is certain both from an external and internal point of view as opposed to the simple grasping of a truth from an external viewpoint, was thus replaced in the Almohad doctrine by the distinction between 'science' and 'plain practice'. As we shall see, the criteria of science which drew upon pure reason in fact went beyond a strictly Islamic framework.

Thus Almohadism in its most consistent form, within the limits of Islam, constituted a rational ordering of the solutions to different problems advanced by the various schools of law. We will find the same to be true of Ibn Rushd's legal works. Almohad *fiqh*, combining its own very particular intellectual bent with practical solutions close to those of the other schools — if not actually borrowed from them — was to continue as a school amongst others until after the fall of the Almohad empire. It was taught in North Africa until the eighth/fourteenth century, disappearing with the spread of a certain intermingling between the traditions.

While the Almoravids were moved by a lurking fear of the disintegration of the Muslim world, especially in the face of the Christian thrust, the Almohads were motivated by an intellectual need with all the rigour that this implied. In the face of historical vicissitudes, the Law represented a structure which could ensure the preservation of the Muslim edifice, and those in power were its guardians. Keeping within this overall schema, the Almohads simply endowed the concepts of Law and Power with a different content. However, what was in theory just a doctrinal problem was complicated by the fact that the struggle between the two dynasties necessitated the participation of the masses for whom, if

INTRODUCTION

they were to gain a hold, the doctrines would have to be transformed into myths capable of stirring the passions, and even reduced to caricatural slogans.

We can see the falsification this process entailed in one of the principal points of Almohad propaganda against the Almoravids. The Almohads exploited the condemnation of Ghazali's works as an indication of Almoravid narrow-mindedness. From this grew up the legend according to which Ghazali himself asked Ibn Tumart to avenge him for this condemnation. This is not only impossible in chronological terms, but also by turning these figures into symbols it denied the genuine influence Ghazali had in al-Andalus at the time of the Almoravids.

It was in fact his pupil Abu Bakr b. al-Arabi who was the first in Spain to bring up the problem of consultations founded on local traditions. The debate continued, but at all events it was from within Andalusian legal circles that the influence of Ghazali caused this question to be raised and not as a result of the imposition of a theological doctrine from outside.

There are other examples which could serve to illustrate the falsity of Almohad propaganda. All underline the difficulty of gaining a hold on the masses by means of a purely intellectual doctrine. Ibn Tumart was aware of this and, besides a profession of faith ('aqida) which as we shall see is of a highly philosophical character and was reserved for the elite, he published two 'spiritual guides' (murshidat) pitched at a much lower level than the profession and differing from one another.

The first reduces philosophical reasoning to the simple principle of the necessary existence of God and develops its religious implications in the balanced style common to this kind of text – contemplation of the nature of God, what he is and what he could not be. This piece is a form of prayer but fairly complex and, according to the chroniclers, more elevated than that generally used by the Mahdi (guide). The latter contained no reference to speculation of any kind and simply reaffirmed submission to God and requested His help in following the true path.

The second spiritual guide was simply an *aide-memoire* for the masses stating: 'Every (Muslim) of legal responsibility must know that . . . .'. Koranic quotations were used more frequently and all logical sequence dispensed with, even on the level of doctrinal consequences, in favour of sonorous turns of phrase. Other works of indoctrination confirm the abandonment of the common herd to a

15

credo they were supposed to recite without question or enquiry. Two 'laudations', doubtless very diluted since both are known also through a medieval Latin translation, served purely to emphasise the transcendence and incomprehensibility of God and to warn against all speculation concerning Him. Everything was subordinated to form and its persuasive powers. Finally, the 'Letters to the Community' simply exhorted the audience to fulfil the duties of Islam and directed a polemic against the Almoravids accusing them of anthropomorphism.

As well as drawing a strong distinction between the elite, for whom intelligence and reasoning were to play an important role, and the masses who had only to 'learn' their credo, Almohadism rested on the idea that it is through belief that the community defines itself. From this stemmed the rejection of authority deemed unworthy and the accusation of polytheism directed against other forms of Islam.

Within the community on the other hand an entire hierarchy was devised based upon the degree of adherence to the doctrine. It is known that Ibn Tumart began his activities as leader of a community with what was known as *tamyiz* – the establishment of an order of pre-eminence between the tribes rallied to his cause and of a strict hierarchy within each one. This division was initially a military one setting out a battle order, but through the enactment of theatrical ritual came to signify an affirmation of support for the cause.

After the tribes of the father and mother of the Mahdi respectively, came the Hintata who were first to have rallied. This hierarchy was highly complex so as to embrace various factors related to Berber social structure or linked to the practice of Holy War, and has now disappeared without trace.[5] However, as it relates to Ibn Rushd, this outline enables us to place him in the group of those close to the rulers, not only through accidents of individual promotion but also within the framework of the collective ideology itself.

In practice, when the movement spread beyond the southern region of Morocco the new conquests were attached to each of the initial classifications so as to unite the more uncertain elements around a faithful core. Eventually, after it expanded beyond the limits of exclusively Berber territory, every employee of the Makhzen from the highest to the lowest was attached to one or other of these groups.

INTRODUCTION

The various Almohad rulers firmly upheld the religious significance of their authority. The break with the Abbasid caliphate had been a reality for three quarters of a century and official letters clearly stated that authority was passed directly from the Prophet to the Mahdi and then to his dynasty of caliphs. The tone of the letters, abounding with propitiatory formulae, differed strongly from that of previous regimes.

Despite these measures, the doctrinal edifice was scarcely able to resist the pressures of reality. Holy wars had previously been waged against Muslims. However, that conducted by the Almohads to gain power rested not upon moral objections but upon the accusation of anthropomorphism associated with the kind of readings primarily undertaken by the Malikis, and consequently with the slavish imitation of the authorities of that school. It was therefore necessary to replace this with doctrine of obedience to the Mahdi. Failure to remain faithful to the Revelation thus became synonymous with infidelity to an individual and the group which upheld him.

Although deemed 'impeccable', the Almohad imam was not the same as the imam of the Shi'ites who had the function of Revelation. In this sphere his role was reduced to the interpretation of ambiguous Koranic verses by the allegorical method and in accordance with both the eternal profession of faith and the positive elaboration of the Law. His essential role was that of politico-religious leader to whom was due absolute obedience and the imitation of his actions. This distinction, however real, nevertheless went unperceived by the masses who confused the Almohad imam with that of the Shi'ites, with all the risks of suspicions of heresy that this entailed. The downgrading of the concept was to culminate a century later in the repudiation of the Almohad doctrine which was re-established for a period but was ultimately doomed to disappear along with the rule of the dynasty.

Such problems help explain why thinkers were the only ones who could be seriously influenced by Almohadism. In it there were certain features similar to the questions which occupied the minds of Andalusian thinkers. Thus Ibn Bajja who knew nothing of this movement had, in the course of a work primarily concerned with metaphysics, already made various allusions to the need for moral reform within Spain and had criticised the luxurious ways and attitudes of the aristocracy not only at the time of the taifa kings but also under the Almoravids.

17

However, the association with *Falsafa* was not as inevitable as the subsequent links between the Almohad powers and the philosophers might lead us to believe. It was Malik b. Wuhayb himself who, on his summons to Marrakesh to become councillor to the Almohad ruler, recommended that he put Ibn Tumart to death. The latter had recently returned from the East where he had drawn attention to himself by his zealous censorship of morals and of the regime.

Later the famous Eastern traditionalist Ibn Taymiya was to detect a profound resemblance between the concept of the divine essence in *Falsafa* and in Almohadism. However, Ibn Tumart's real meaning is difficult to pin down. Muslim interpreters have followed their usual approach in attempting to associate it with pre-existing politico-religious movements (Mutazilism, Ash'arism, shi'ism and in particular Ismailism, *Falsafa*) but at the cost of drawing unsustainable parallels and without ever reaching a consensus. A more enlightening approach is to seek the meaning of this thought in the author's early formative period preceding even his move to Cordoba and the East.

A Berber educated in the environment Islamized by secessionist Khariji movements, Ibn Tumart's doctrine displays, beyond a sentimental attachment to Sunnism resulting from Alawite activities in the Maghreb, the fundamental elements of Kharijism. These arose within a continuation of a specific trend espoused by the Berber intelligentsia in direct opposition to the Berber masses with their predilection for the forces of magic. This line of thought had begun with the Punic notion of a great national God, master of all, and was developed by Roman, pagan thinkers into a form of henotheism and then a particularly strict form of monotheism with Judaism, Christianity and Islam. With its polemic expressly directed against the cult of spirits, this movement found much to its taste in the Khariji doctrines which fought all distinctions between the attributes of God and affirmed the necessity of His decrees as supreme, independent and unsusceptible to manipulation by the workings of magic.

On this informal basis the man who was to become the guide (*mahdi*) of the Almohads (from *al-Muwahidun*, meaning believers in divine unicity) elaborated a wholly rational theology irresistibly reminiscent of the ontological argument formulated some years earlier in the Christian world by St Anselm. Starting out from the single criterion of purity of intention Ibn Tumart progressed

INTRODUCTION

towards a God proved purely in accordance with the rules of reason through a series of conditions in which 'divine promises and threats' formed a pivot around which was constructed a rational theology and Islam itself.

The Almohad profession of faith will be examined in greater detail in Ch.2. It suffices here to point out that Almohadism was a fusion of a theology based on the analysis of the problem of inference and positing the existence of an Absolute Being, with a practical philosophy which conformed quite naturally to the forms of Islamic law and which hung entirely upon the notion of divine transcendence. Hence we can see the division between the sphere of faith which was purely rational and that of practice which followed almost wholly positive methods.

It was inevitable that a system of thought so perfectly sculpted and in which the only role of Revelation was to provide content for a framework deduced wholly in accordance with the dictates of reason should remain impenetrable to the spirits of the age. Thus the Almohad propagandists, who were more concerned with effectiveness than respect for the intellectual approach of the Mahdi, proceeded to render it accessible by breaking it down into propositions and attitudes, relating the former to existing movements and interpreting the latter as a form of polemic.

It was the struggle to seize power from the Almoravids that caused parallels to be drawn between, on the one hand, the works of Ghazali which the Almoravids had condemned and, on the other, the use of rational proofs as dogma and allegorical interpretation of the Revelation which was likened to the practices of *Kalam*, and insistence on the sources of Law which was related to Ghazali's treatises on juridical methodology, and so forth.

The extreme density but subsequently very limited scope of the Almohad profession of faith, which constituted the only truly doctrinal work, explains why these parallels were not generally enlarged upon and why there was ample room for confusion. As a result there grew up a profusion of tales telling how Ghazali charged Ibn Tumart with the task of avenging him and once in power acting as propagandist for the works of his supposed master.

In reality, the thought of the Berber scholar Ibn Tumart constituted an implicit rebuttal of the thought of the Eastern thinker Ghazali. He opposed syncretism with an austere doctrine drawn solely from the analysis of concepts. He rejected the mystics' 'science of the heart' and replaced contemplation of the divine names with submission to the Absolute Being whose attributes were simple descriptions created by Himself.

Despite the impossibility of fitting it into the Islamic tradition, Almohadism was nevertheless fundamentally Muslim in character both as a result of its Khariji roots and through its complete integration of the material of the Revelation with the philosophical approach it had formulated. While it may not have placed the Text (*Nas*) foremost and though it cannot be reduced to a commentary on the Revelation filled with heterogeneous elements, it would nevertheless be just as arbitrary to leave it out of a history of Islamic thought as it would to exclude part of the works of Saint Anselm from Christian thought.

It was nevertheless the case that such a system of thought could only exert an influence on certain approaches which were marginal, in terms of numbers, by virtue of their fundamental rationalism. Hence for certain minds to be ready to embrace it, it was vital that they find some sort of support from within the intellectual history of the Muslim world. This support was provided by *Falsafa* which, though espoused by a small minority compared to other currents of Islamic thought, nevertheless boasted a degree of antiquity.

Hence the historical link between Andalusian *Falsafa* and the political situation should not be underestimated. Indeed there was a vigorous revival in Spanish intellectual life under the new dynasty. Of the first Almohad caliph 'Abd al-Mu'min the chroniclers have left little more than the image of a conqueror. However, while the political talents of his successor Yusuf are not to be underrated, it was the reputation of this caliph as a true scholar comparable to the Ummayad ruler al-Hakam II that spread as far as the Muslim East.

It was he who made Seville the new capital of al-Andalus, bedecked with magnificent monuments of which the Giralda and remaining parts of the Alcazar provide a doubtless pale image. Despite its partial disfigurement during the sixteenth century, the Giralda nevertheless remains a remarkable artistic example of Almohad ideology incorporated in plastic form with its large-scale ornamentation combining big, unfilled geometric forms with surfaces finely decorated with brick filigree work, elegant windows piercing walls 2.5 m thick, and a frieze of small columns crowning the summit.

Almohadism constituted a 'state of mind' shaped by the

INTRODUCTION

convergence of several highly heterogeneous currents: Ibn Bajja's continuation of the work of *Falsafa*, opposed both to a purely 'cultural' conception of speculation and to the Ghazalian perspective; the imposition of rationalizing reform on the Western part of the Muslim world; and to these should now be added a final element constituted by the very marked development of the Andalusian scientific approach away from its pragmatic character and towards a veritable cult of systematization.

Muslim civilization had developed a vast body of practical science that might be described as 'spontaneous', in other words related to the practical concerns of existence. It included pharmacology, a knowledge of chemistry necessary to combat dishonest practice in the market place, almanacs and so forth. However, in contrast to the contempt for speculative thought that may have existed in Spain outside Islamic culture, the oriental Muslims immediately recognised its (albeit distinctly relative) scientific tradition. In the sixth/twelfth century, the Syrian chronicler Ibn 'Asakir recalled that Tariq, the conqueror of the peninsula, returned from his campaigns with Bibles and works on alchemy and the natural sciences.

This empirical knowledge seldom led on to a more organized knowledge. Indeed the distinction was barely even recognised from the earliest days of Andalusian science when, with somewhat haphazard enthusiasm, the geographers, astronomers and doctors vied to accumulate knowledge, whether derived from ancient writers or arising from the recent discoveries of practice.

Agronomy was the only field to begin with a purely theoretical phase. However, it also signalled a general rethinking in the sciences accomplished by means of a double rupture. Initially this involved a return beyond the authors of late antiquity to an approach which established an atmosphere that might be described as truly Aristotelian and which broke from the cult of those in power. In the second phase, theory regained its standing and knowledge was reorganized in an attempt at a new synthesis in which the contributions of experience were integrated with the ancient knowledge that they had helped refine and purify. This was also visible in the field of geography, notably with al-Idrisi.

However, these sciences remained primarily practical in aim if not in structure. They were not carried on into any fundamental speculation, although in their content there was no lack of speculative elements inherited from antiquity. The situation was different with regard to knowledge of the universe, and that universe in microcosm that the medievals saw in the human body. Thus when this rethinking of all the sciences was taking place, a split emerged between the requirements of practice – which continued to consist in the accumulation of knowledge – and the work of the true scholar, a figure increasingly removed from the populace and exhibiting a growing desire to follow studies leading to an all-embracing vision.

In a sense, the disinterested pursuit of knowledge barely existed beyond the work of a few individuals engaged solely in the elaboration of a discipline of practical origins such as accountancy. In all other instances, knowledge either led exclusively to professional practice or served as a vehicle for a particular religious or philosophical objective.

The intellectual and social gap between these two approaches was filled in due course by the first popular speculations of the Ummayad period (alchemy, neoplatonism popularized by the school of Ibn Masarra, etc.). At times these were pursued openly in the mystical environment of the brotherhoods or amongst individuals, in some cases with an overt political aim (as, for example, with Ibn Barrajan and Ibn Qaoyí – Sufis who rebelled against the Almoravids). Most often, however, they were practised as forms of elitism, elevating the initiate above the common herd through a knowledge that could provide the key to both the world of phenomena and of the invisible, and ultimately to God Himself.

We will limit ourselves here to the consideration of science that developed along speculative lines while remaining anchored in rational experiment. However, this is itself not entirely neutral, as proved by the fluctuating importance attached to particular sciences at different times. Thus the exact sciences suffered considerably less than the natural sciences as a result of the upheavals of the crisis of the caliphate at the beginning of the fifth/ eleventh century. Many of the great figures in the exact sciences produced their work during this period when the natural sciences were in rapid decline, and a greater number of scholars continued to work in the exact sciences during the Taifa period.

The sciences as a whole underwent a revival at the beginning of the Almoravid period, although this was more marked in the exact sciences. After another period of eclipse, however, it was the natural sciences that came to the fore with the start of the Almohad period, and this tendency strengthened in subsequent

INTRODUCTION

years. This overall Andalusian pattern was repeated in Cordoba and Seville with certain variations, including a greater emphasis on the exact sciences in Cordoba under the Almohads and a greater concentration of natural scientists in Seville towards the end of the Almohad era.

The Almohad period thus brought a reversal of perspectives. Previously, the two branches of science had been practised in fairly close relation to one another, the natural sciences also being combined with the study of *adab* (belles-lettres) and to a lesser extent that of the prophetic traditions, law, poetry and Arabic language. There was virtually no link with theology and none at all with philosophy. The exact sciences were allied more closely with the study of Arabic than with the natural sciences, then with Law, and to a much more limited degree with *adab*. While there was a similar lack of connection with philosophy, they were linked with theology almost as closely as with the other religious and literary disciplines.

With the rise of Almohadism, however, the link between the two fields dissolved almost completely. The natural sciences were practised primarily along with *adab*, Arabic language and the traditions, and began to be more closely linked with the basics of Law and with philosophy.

The exact sciences, which were on the decline, no longer had any particularly strong links except with the study of the Koran, besides a very limited extension into the speculative religious disciplines. While the philosophers incorporated astronomy in their investigations, the mathematicians seldom sought to widen their sphere of practice. Hence there was a movement away from a global scientific culture fitting into the overall Islamic cultural context, towards a speculative option that revolved primarily around the study of man and the world.

In this too the work of Ibn Bajja marked a decisive stage, if not for the scientific community of the peninsula as a whole, at least for the tendency with which Ibn Rushd was to align himself. For example, in his *Treatise on plants* Ibn Bajja did not study each one on its own, since he considered exhaustive enumeration an impossible task. Instead he started by setting out the characteristics common to the entire plant kingdom together with their causes in accordance with Aristotelian theory, then presented the main distinctions between them. The plants listed thus only appeared as examples of these categories, organized according to

23

entirely external criteria – possession or lack of roots, aquatic or terrestrial, parasitic or non-parasitic, etc. This was particularly true where the divisions became finest – dimensions of the root and foliage, lifespan, edibility, etc.

In his study of the common characteristics of plants Ibn Bajja remained faithful to Aristotle, except on the question of sexual reproduction in plants where he accepted the hypothesis but in a purely metaphorical sense. Similarly, while agreeing with Aristotle in accepting mobility and sensitivity as the criteria distinguishing vegetable from animal, a number of specific observations led him to formulate doubts regarding the divisions between the different kingdoms. He recognised that certain plants can react to external stimuli, described how certain aquatic plants such as the water-lily open and close their flowers at different times of day, and finally pointed to the phenomenon of parasitic and aquatic plants without roots.

He overcame these difficulties by attributing the first phenomenon to purely physico-chemical mechanisms reconcilable with Aristotelian theory on the properties of the elements, and by refusing to take the others as proof of localized movement in plants. While thus stopping short of fundamental investigations into the problems of evolutionism, he nevertheless explicitly set out the hypothesis that there is no fundamental difference between the various kingdoms – mineral and vegetable, animal and human – resting his proof on the ambiguous cases represented by the starfish, ostrich and the monkey, respectively. This idea was later taken up by Ibn Tufayl (d. 581/1185–6) who envisaged the continuous development of organisms starting with elementary forms arising out of 'natural heat' and moving up through vegetable life and then motor, sensory and finally rational forms.

However, it is not here that the essential significance of his philosophical investigations into the plant kingdom lies. Moreover, Ibn Tufayl was thinking far more of the animal kingdom when he developed his theory. The point of Ibn Bajja's outline is to demonstrate the need to look into the causes of every property, whatever it may be, from a rigorously deterministic standpoint ('absence of cause of existence is the cause of privation' (Asin Palacios, 'Avempace Botanico', pp.271/289)), distinguishing only between that necessary for existence and that which contributes to the perfection of the being. The exclusive reliance in this on the Aristotelian system can be explained by the lack of sophistication

INTRODUCTION

of contemporary research, and even more by the diffuse nature of these investigations. A century later Albertus Magnus, who was strongly influenced by the work of Ibn Bajja, drew on a greater amount of documentation and personal observations, and in his *De vegetabilibus aut plantis* was able to embark on the realization of Ibn Bajja's project.

Thus three main interconnecting currents emerge: a speculative approach introduced fairly late, and attempted through 'cultural' syncretism, was partially formalized by Ibn Bajja who set out the basic problematic. Eastern *Falsafa* had been elaborated in such a way that Ghazali had been able to produce a synthesis of it before refuting it wholesale – the only examples he was unable to include, in particular Abu-l-Barakat al-Baghdadi and Abu Bakr al-Razi, had no influence in al-Andalus. It was thus possible to an extent to reconsider the question from the start. Ibn Bajja also pushed scientific practice in a certain direction, accentuating a tendency which was already emerging in somewhat diffuse fashion. The correlation with a rationalizing religious framework such as Almohadism thus appears self-evident.

However, the situation was not nearly so simple, and older tendencies persisted to a considerable extent – as witnessed by the work of Ibn Tufayl which represented an intermediate stage between that of Ibn Bajja, who made the initial exploratory inroads, and that of Ibn Rushd who clearly indicated the options which presented themselves.

Almost nothing is known of the upbringing and education of Ibn Tufayl. He was born in Guadix in the early years of the sixth/twelfth century and appears to have lived initially in Granada. He must then have received his education either in Seville or Cordoba or both, since he is sometimes referred to as al-Qurtubi or al-Ishbili. He admits to never having come into direct contact with Ibn Bajja and, although he could have had some connections with Malik b. Wuhayb or even Ibn al-Imam in Seville, he claims no knowledge of their works.

He devoted himself to both medicine and politics in the service of the Almohads. He also worked as propagandist for the dynasty, unhindered by scruples as to the techniques he employed. We have a political poem of his written for the purpose of enlisting Arab tribes into the armies of his master. The poem lacks neither traditional Arab themes (exultation of martial glory, the privileged status of the tribe of Qays), nor slogans relating to the Almohad cause which may consist of flagrant lies (for example, regarding the Qaysite origins of Ibn Tumart and his caliphs).

Despite his highly philosophical background, Ibn Tufayl ultimately claimed Ghazali as the 'father' of Almohadism. He excused his contradictions arguing that he addressed himself to audiences of different levels in his various works. According to Ibn Tufayl, the answer to these contradictions was to be found in the esoteric works, although none of the works that had reached Spain belonged to this category. This enabled Ibn Tufayl to refer directly to Ibn Sina. The critique against him formulated in the exoteric works of Ghazali was overcome by reference to his 'illuminating wisdom'. The master had stated that there is no contradiction between that which is attained through reason and that reached through enlightenment, the latter differing only in its greater clarity. He also emphasised that the true meaning of his interpretation of Aristotle lay not in literal comprehension but in its esoteric interpretation – hence Ibn Tufayl's borrowing of the title of a narrative of Ibn Sina which was far shorter than his own and difficult to interpret. Moreover, while the two works have little in common on the level of narrative – Ibn Tufayl drew inspiration for his work from an Arab legend – the full title nevertheless declares the work to be an exposition of the 'secrets of illuminating wisdom' (*Risala Hayy ibn Yaqzan fi asrar al-Hikmat al-Mushriqiya*).

Ibn Tufayl does not limit himself to referring to the thoughts of Ghazali and Ibn Sina 'relating one to the other'. He also claims to relate 'both of them to opinions which have arisen in our own era and are being eagerly adopted by those who profess the pursuit of philosophy' (ed.Gauthier, p.16). Why should he seek such support from writers to whom he does not even explicitly refer? Ibn Bajja, who is mentioned by name elsewhere, had described illumination as an illusion, and denied that Ghazali achieved the level he claimed. Ibn Tufayl defended him on the grounds that Ibn Bajja's work had remained unfinished, suggesting that his work was not unique in being questionable, and that Ibn Bajja should have hesitated before going to such an extreme in view of his own contradictions, in particular concerning his personal ethics. He also invokes a passage from Ibn Bajja's *Treatise on the union of the Agent Intellect with man* where Ibn Bajja goes so far as to speak of the 'hidden sense' which transforms the scientific approach in order for it to pass from the physical world into divine realities.

INTRODUCTION

Such manipulation would not have been sufficient in itself. Indeed, Ibn Tufayl's concern was not to seek justification for his approach in the work of his predecessor, but rather to integrate it with his own thought to the extent that it too was justified by its correspondence to the contemporary ideology to which he adhered, i.e. Almohadism.

Like Ibn Tumart, though independently of him and in a completely different way, Ibn Bajja envisaged reason rising by its own powers to the level of the Absolute Being. Hence, though unfinished, his philosophy can be exploited both for its approach (the hero of Ibn Tufayl's novel can be taken as the epitome of Ibn Bajja's 'solitary'), and also for the material with which it deals.

However, underlying all this, the theology of Ibn Tumart is reiterated: the subject quite independently elevates itself through reflection upon the world, itself and its own genesis to the idea of the Creator through the necessary principle which infers from a product the existence of a producer. It is reason alone that enables the attainment of knowledge of the positive and negative attributes, and the idea that the former imply the latter so that they possess no corporeal qualities, in particular mutiplicity, and that leads to the conclusion that the positive attributes all revert to a single notion, which is its very essence.

The second character of the novel, Asal, who confronts concrete religion with the experience of the pure subject represented by Hayy, sanctions the fusion of Islam with rational theology stating that

> all the traditions of its religious Law relating to God, Great and Mighty, to his angels, his books, his envoys, the last day, to his paradise and to the fire (of Hell) (are) symbols of what Hayy Ibn Yaqzan perceived and laid bare. . . . He witnessed the establishment of reconciliation between reason and tradition; the paths of allegorical interpretation opened up to him; there remained in the divine Law nothing difficult which he could not understand, nothing closed which did not open, nothing obscure which did not become clear. (p.106)

It is not insignificant that these various elements should have been brought together in a single literary work. Clothing the austere thought of the Berber Mahdi with all the scientific, cosmological, psychological and metaphysical elements of Andalusian civilization, Ibn Tufayl rediscovered the tradition of *adab*, which acted as an expression of culture whatever its content. Yet it has also been remarked that the two greatest works of Andalusian prose – Ibn Hazm's *Collar of the dove* and Ibn Tufayl's *Hayy Ibn Yaqzan* are products of writer-philosophers, and indeed above all, philosophers. It is in the *Collar of the dove* that Ibn Hazm's literalism yields most to neoplatonic themes.

Hence the literary act constituted a summons to a symbolic world which rounded out the dry exercise of reason. Doubtless the quality of the resulting work sprang from the fact that this summons was born of experience: love in the case of Ibn Hazm, and illumination extending the exercise of reason in the case of Ibn Tufayl. The latter, however, was aware of his 'lack of rigour in demonstration' and aimed only to 'give an approximate idea (of his own experience) so as to inspire a burning desire to set out upon the path' (p.114).

Thus, while standing at the juncture of the three intellectual currents identified above, Ibn Tufayl only helped complicate the situation, accentuating the syncretism of Eastern *Falsafa*. This explains the radical position taken by Ibn Rushd despite his personal links with Ibn Tufayl. The return to Aristotle advocated by the younger scholar was not motivated simply by the occasional suggestions which we will come to in due course, nor even by a particular attraction exerted by Aristotle. Rather, it provided a fundamental response to a need – the need to develop every field of knowledge in a coherent manner so as adequately to fill in the gaps and insufficiencies in the Andalusian tradition, moving beyond the errors and tentative gropings of the brief period of intellectual development from the fourth/tenth century until the beginning of the sixth/twelfth century.

Ibn Rushd's basic approach is identical to that of the first editors of Aristotle's work. This complex body of thought which Aristotle had seldom had the chance to synthesize at a later stage (with the exception of the *Physics* and the *Soul*), was transformed by Andronicus of Rhodes and his successors into a model of systematization. This can be attributed to the successive crises of the Hellenistic period which made it necessary to endow the spirit of the work with its own framework and precise avenues of investigation. It is impossible to understand the work of Ibn Rushd, not only his Aristotelian commentaries, but also his medical works, his intellectual writings in support of Almohadism and even his work as a jurist, if one does not bear in mind his

INTRODUCTION

desire not only to construct a system but to establish the field of rationality.

BIOGRAPHY AND FAMILY BACKGROUND

Not only were the Banu Rushd a family of prominent jurists, as already mentioned, but they were also involved in politics. Moreover, these two spheres of activity were linked and merit closer examination.

When the Almoravids established themselves in Spain towards the end of the fifth/eleventh century, they treated it as conquered territory. The Berber military presence was unpleasantly reminiscent to the Cordobans of the troubles that had arisen at the beginning of the century with the ending of the Ummayad caliphate. The feelings of unrest that were stirred up culminated in 515/1121 with the revolt of the capital and the sacking of the governor's palace.

When the ruler arrived with his army, the religious leaders formed a delegation under Abu-l-Walid Muhammad b. Rushd, grandfather and namesake of the philosopher. The delegation set forth a defence of the people and gained a pardon from the prince who limited himself to demanding compensation for material damages.

Despite this success Ibn Rushd, who had been appointed by the sovereign, stepped down and the people obtained the re-instatement of the man he had replaced. The ruler, however, appointed as governor a member of one of the leading Berber families, and ten years later his own son took the position. This policy of counterbalance came to an end in 532/1137 when the Almonavid ruler re-imposed one of his own supporters as Qadi – the new occupant of the post being none other than Ibn Rushd's son, Abu-l-Qasim Ahmad.

When in their turn the Almohads were making inroads into Spain (541/1145–6), the people of Cordoba took advantage of the absence of the governor who had left the city to fight the rebels, in order to mount a revolt against him and, doubtless, against the Qadi associated with him.

The first of the Banu Rushd were therefore closely linked with the ruling powers and consequently with the Almoravid ideology. Abu-l-Walid al-Jadd ('the grandfather') left several famous *fatawi* (legal opinions) relating to his political career. One dealt with an apparently minor point but one which was to play a major role in the propaganda justifying civil war. It concerned the wearing of the veil (*litham*) by the Almoravids as a mark of fidelity to the Saharan origins of their movement, while their women went unveiled through a survival of matriarchal Berber practice. Ibn Rushd declared the first practice legitimate except during the execution of religious duties.

On a more important and far-reaching point, the establishment of the Almoravids in an atmosphere of holy war encouraged the general diffusion of an intolerance which had hitherto only manifested itself on a sporadic basis. In particular, this led to the wholesale departure of Christian Mozarabs who had been peaceful and consenting subjects of the Muslim state since the middle of the fourth/tenth century. In the year of his death (520/1126) although he now only held the office of Qadi, Abu-l-Walid b. Rushd ordered the deportation to the Maghreb of a large number of those Mozarabs who remained in Spain, his aim being to pre-empt the emergence of a 'fifth column' sympathetic to the enemies in the north.

Ibn Rushd emerges as both servile and intolerant if viewed solely on the basis of these examples (though they do serve to illustrate the doctrinal extension of his political involvement). However, it should also be pointed out that he was the author of a *Bayan* (explanation) which is the most famous commentary ever written on the *'Utbiya*, a collection of *responsa* to specific cases (*masa'il*) compiled in the third/ninth century by the Andalusian al-'Utbi. His fidelity in this work to the purest Maliki tradition of al-Andalus offsets the caricatural image of the Almoravids traditionally put forward.

As we have seen, the real picture of the Almoravids is not as simple as has been made out – and the same is true of Ibn Rushd. In fact he is quoted by the biographers as a recognized specialist in the field of juridical methodology and the study of the various legal solutions put forward by the major schools of Law (*Ikhtilaf*).

To give one example illustrative of his standpoint: in a *fatwa* he challenged the evidence of the literalist jurists (*Zahiris*) who nevertheless enjoyed a high reputation and were widely respected. He justified this on the grounds that their rejection of reasoning by analogy (*qiyas*) as one of the theoretical foundations of legislation amounted to innovation (*bid'a*). Following the lines of the fifth/eleventh-century reform of the school, reasoning by analogy –

INTRODUCTION

which thus acquired a status denied by early Maliki thought – was based not on reason but justified by the sole authority of the Revelation. In this, therefore, he came very close to Almohadism.

His grandson Abu-l-Walid Muhammad ibn Ahmad al-Hafiz was born in Cordoba in 520/1126, the same year as the death of his famous grandfather. He had a standard training and was initially better known to the Andalusian biographers as a jurist than as a scholar and philosopher. Ibn al-Abbar even emphasised his activities as a scholar of the Tradition, though recognising elsewhere that he preferred the speculative aspect to the simple transmission of information.

Despite his family's prominent links with the Almoravid regime, Ibn Rushd openly sided with the Almohads. In view of what we have seen this need not necessarily be attributed to opportunism, since the intellectual stance of his grandfather had already paved the way for such a shift. In fact opting for the new regime was not as profitable a move as it might appear, at least in the early stages. In contrast to Ibn Tufayl who settled in the Maghreb, Ibn Rushd visited it apparently fairly frequently but only temporarily. Essentially he stayed in al-Andalus praising its charms and pleasant climate.

However, the country lamented the passing of the Almoravids and clung to a traditionalist outlook. The renewal of official personnel outside strictly political and administrative circles only took place there after some twenty years once the change of regime was complete. Moreover, the process was not a thorough one, and left a small nucleus of those loyal to the regime co-existing with a large body of ulema who were more reluctant in their support. This second group had managed to effect a reconciliation between their own tradition and the new ideology that significantly attenuated the force of the latter. The final disgrace of Ibn Rushd was a clear demonstration of the ill-feeling with which he was certainly viewed by his countrymen – just like his father and grandfather before him, despite the change of regime.

However, it was only indirectly through the intervention of Ibn Tufayl that Ibn Rushd became linked with the ruling regime. His relationship with Ibn Tufayl was complex. It is generally thought that the latter wrote his philosophical novel fairly late in life, perhaps only a few years before his death in 581/1185. In fact it was certainly before 575/1179, the year in which Ibn Rushd produced his most distinctive works, since Ibn Tufayl declared of his contemporaries that none had yet shown proof of their abilities.

Yet it was considerably earlier that the famous episode took place when the younger scholar was presented to the Almohad Sultan under his auspices. The account of the chronicler al-Marrakushi, based on the eyewitness report of Abu Bakr Bundud of Cordoba and giving the actual words of Ibn Rushd, is cited in all the histories of Arab philosophy. It tells how Ibn Tufayl sang the praises of his friend whereupon the Sultan, after enquiring about Ibn Rushd's family, asked straight out: 'What is the opinion of the philosophers on the skies? Are they made of eternal substance or did they have a beginning?' Ibn Rushd was disconcerted and evaded the question, but the Sultan and Ibn Tufayl began discussing the subject in front of him in highly erudite fashion and gradually succeeded in drawing him into the discussion.

On another occasion, Ibn Tufayl confided to him a reflection expressed by someone described without further specification as 'the prince of believers': 'Would to God that we could find someone willing to make a commentary upon (the) works (of Aristotle) and explain their meaning clearly so as to render them accessible to men!' Feeling himself too old and too busy to undertake this task, Ibn Tufayl charged Ibn Rushd with its execution.

The only information about the philosophical education of the young Ibn Rushd is given by the Eastern medical historian Ibn Abi Usaybi'a in a biography of one of his teachers in this field, Abu Ja'far ibn Harun de Trujillo, who was doctor to Abu Ya'qub Yusuf when he was still governor of Seville. He depicts Ibn Harun as possessing a perfect knowledge of the philosophical sciences and the works in which they were set out, in addition to being well-versed in the works of Aristotle and other ancient philosophers. No other links have been found connecting Ibn Rushd with contemporary philosophical circles, and it was just as much through medicine that he came into contact with Ibn Tufayl, exchanging letters with him on this subject and replacing him as physician to the Sultan in 578/1182.

The intervention of the Sultan was undoubtedly decisive in his career. However, the anecdotes recounted above arouse a number of questions. Our knowledge of the chronology of Ibn Rushd's works and of the prominence he gained in the hierarchy through his successive appointments as Qadi, makes it necessary for us to look

INTRODUCTION

back to a fairly early stage to understand why he needed to be presented to the Sultan and why he believed he could keep his study of philosophy secret.

It is just feasible to propose 548/1153 as the year Ibn Rushd was presented to the Sultan (in which case the ruler would have been 'Abd al-Mu'min) since this was the year when he was in Marrakesh helping with the reform of education. However, there is too long a period between this date and the composition of the first commentaries for it also to have been the year in which Ibn Rushd was advised to devote himself to the interpretation of Aristotle. This advice makes better sense if placed in Seville around 554/1159 in the court of Abu Ya'qub Yusuf. The latter had been governor of the city for five years and was to become Sultan three years later, adopting the title of 'Commander of the Faithful' in 564/1168. However, the aforementioned account was produced at a much later date. It is even likely that it was to Abu Ya'qub that Ibn Rushd had been presented shortly before, rather than to his father in 548/1153 in Marrakesh. Although the latter was certainly a cultivated man, the question on the skies is more comprehensible coming from his son who was highly knowledgeable in the sciences, especially medicine, and also in philosophy.

It was he who built up a library in Seville which outshone even that of al-Hakam II. To accomplish this he even went so far as to commandeer private collections in return for lavish compensation. Such plunder is understandable when seen alongside that of his victims, a number of whom had themselves profited from the forced sale of estates caused by the upheavals in order to collect books, mainly on astrology, which were brought to them by the sackload.

It is the Sultan's insistence on the works of Aristotle that constitutes the newest phenomenon. Previous rulers had quite frequently shown interest in philosophy as a branch of culture. As early as the the fourth/tenth century the 'master of the palace' al-Mansur', famous for the violent inquisition he unleashed against intellectuals in order to win the allegiance of the jurists, himself pursued a private interest in the subject. The discussion of the skies arose within an eclectic culture which since the time of al-Hakam II had become widespread in circles of a not strictly legalistic outlook.

However, the Almohad ruler was no longer content with a review of the various answers put forward as resolutions to the

IBN RUSHD (AVERROES)

major issues. He now also specified a precise orientation. It appears that Ibn Tufayl was not tempted by this undertaking (if indeed it was he who acted as intermediary and not, for example, Ibn Harun who was physician to Abu Ya'qub and teacher to Ibn Rushd). He viewed the exoteric exposition of Aristotle as a doubtless valuable stage – but merely a stage – on the road to enlightenment. Ibn Rushd's enthusiastic acceptance, on the other hand, suggests a profound agreement with his master's perspective. This agreement can be seen in the impact of Ibn Tumart's doctrines on his own thinking, manifested in a theological rationalism preliminary to philosophical research which is considered the ultimate embodiment of 'reason'.

However, the contemporary milieu was not one in which philosophy enjoyed a high status. Hence, it was as a jurist that Ibn Rushd was obliged to carry out his activities. In 565/1169 he was appointed Qadi of Seville, which had become the capital of al-Andalus. Two years later he returned to Cordoba as Qadi, while undertaking a number of trips to Seville and Marrakesh. He was appointed Qadi of Seville a second time in 575/1179, and three years later became Grand Qadi of Cordoba. Several months prior to this he had succeeded Ibn Tufayl as personal physician to the Sultan. When Abu Yusuf Ya'qub (al-Mansur), brother to the previous Sultan, ascended the throne in 580/1184, Ibn Rushd spent most of his time attending him and became one of his companions and even a close friend.

All these connections with the Almohads were sanctified by Ibn Rushd's attachment to the class of the Hintata within the hierarchy that supported the system. This was the third most elevated rank, that of 'those who rallied in the first hour'. Its significance can only have been symbolic given that Ibn Rushd's participation in this rally would have been a physical impossibility.

The last famous episode of Ibn Rushd's life is the disgrace which befell him shortly before his death and which he had foreseen in the wake of his unexpected and excessive fortune under the protection of Sultan Ya'qub. This episode is recounted by the chroniclers with numerous details which are also quoted by historians of Arab philosophy following Renan. However, these details are not wholly coherent, and the overall situation at the time should also be taken into account.

In 586/1190 the advance of the Portuguese who had taken Silves and were threatening Seville prompted the Sultan to declare a holy

INTRODUCTION

war. He then had to grapple with unrest in the central Maghreb which he was unable to suppress entirely. Once back in Cordoba, he set off to confront a Christian coalition at Alarcos near Badajoz where he won a resounding victory in 591/1195. This was confirmed shortly after by a new expedition launched from Seville as far as Trujillo, Talavera and Toledo.

However, the Sultan was doubtless aware of the weaknesses of his empire and anxious to restore cohesion, and this led him to revive the practices of the Almoravids. Back in Seville after his second expedition, he sacrificed to the jurists a number of individuals of whom Ibn Rushd and Muhammad b. Ibrahim al-Mahri (al-Usuli) were simply the most famous.

Looking at these two alone, we find their orientations to be highly distinct. While both were specialists in juridical methodology, al-Usuli was most famous for his critical commentary on Ghazali's *Mustasfa*, of which Ibn Rushd produced only a synopsis. He was, in addition, an authority on the Traditions and on *Kalam*, a discipline which was a favourite target of Ibn Rushd. Little is known of his actual philosophy, and the historians limit themselves to noting the linking of their indictments: 'His theories on the sciences of the ancients and those of Ibn Rushd were the object of a famous investigation in Cordoba in 592 (1196), and the people praised his forebearance on this occasion', says Ibn al-Abbar (ed. Cordera, no. 1070).

In fact we need to look beyond the reasons put forward by the chroniclers. These appear childish when they relate to personal causes, and improbable in invoking doctrinal reasons since it is impossible that the Sultan was unfamiliar with the thought of his protégé. Rather it is the geographical situation of the two men that is revealing.

Ibn Rushd was from Cordoba, the 'soft underbelly' of al-Andalus. Al-Mahri, though born of a Sevillian family, came from Bougie in the part of the central Maghreb where rebellion smouldered against the Almohads. Only after 608/1211 did he settle in Spain as Qadi of Murcia, and he ended his career as Qadi of Marrakesh – an indication of his return to favour.

Ibn Rushd was thus the victim of a political gesture, and was sacrificed by the Sultan in order to win over the masses. Moreover, while the ruling regime had attempted a direct doctrinal offensive in al-Andalus in the years 575–6/1179–80, a new tendency was now beginning to emerge which would triumph after the next generation. This no longer focused on securing the acceptance of Almohadism primarily by the elite, but concentrated instead on rendering it acceptable to all by linking it to movements already in existence. Thus the rulers had an interest in accepting such a compromise while discarding those of their followers who were most difficult to link in with it.

Ibn Rushd's disgrace consisted in his exile to Lucena, a small town south of Cordoba. The majority of its inhabitants were Jews who had established an important talmudic school there. However, this was suppressed by the new leaders who simultaneously implemented a policy of forced conversion. This exile was thus doubly insulting since it linked the victim with a group considered inferior by the Muslims, whilst in the eyes of the townspeople he was associated with the persecuting power. Ibn Rushd was subjected to insults and epigrams, some examples of which have been preserved by al-Ansari. He was described as *mutafalsif* – a term on a par with Berkeley's 'minute philosopher' – and on these lines was constructed the term *mutazindiq* meaning 'mediocre heretic'.

He nevertheless continued his work. Moreover, as soon as news of his exile got out the dignitaries of Seville petitioned in his favour. After two or three years the Sultan, who dared not impose him on the Cordobans again, had him brought to his court in Marrakesh where both died a few months later. The most likely date of Ibn Rushd's death is Thursday 9 Safar 595/10 December 1198.

He was initially buried in Marrakesh but his remains were later taken to Cordoba on a mule – their weight being balanced by his works of philosophy. Several of his sons continued in the family tradition and went on to become Qadis, and one became physician to the Sultan.

* * *

Studies of the chronology of Ibn Rushd's works (M. Alonso and N. Morata) have distinguished three periods of production. This is the sequence we will follow here so as best to fulfil the programme of enquiry set out at the beginning. This is preferable to dealing question by question with an Averroist system which does not in fact exist.

(1) In the initial period until 567/1170 Ibn Rushd devoted himself

INTRODUCTION

mainly to the brief commentaries (*jami'*), and from 564/1168 to 571/1175 to the middle commentaries (*talkhis*). The former are introductory works which provided a general presentation of the art of logic, of physical, psychological, scientific and other questions, rather than giving an explanation of Aristotle's own specific logic, physics and so forth. They were intended to enable progression to scientific work elaborated elsewhere by Ibn Rushd. They included a continuous and impersonal commentary on the medical poem of Ibn Sina, then the *Kulliyat* and the treatise *On Theriac* in which Ibn Rushd adopted an original position on the question of therapeutics.

To this he added physics, cosmology, psychology and the natural sciences, this time presented through the work of Aristotle. This work was set out in the middle commentaries in which Ibn Rushd distanced himself from al-Farabi, Ibn Sina, and indeed from his own position in the brief commentaries by setting himself to follow the order of the text. This, however, does not imply servility. In fact he gave his own structure to the text under commentary, highlighting certain passages to the detriment of others, spending time over a particular problem to which Aristotle only attached minor importance and leaving out another to which there was no solution. Finally, he introduced the arguments of other commentators where necessary.

To this we should add his composition of the treatise on Law. This work was of double importance, first because it dealt with the practical aspects of the doctrine of the Almohad mahdi (whereas all Ibn Rushd's other works during this first period were essentially devoted to speculation), and second because it establishes the particular prominence of Ibn Rushd, who was not a marginal figure but rather fully involved in the affairs of the Muslim community. (It is very likely that it was this work that enabled him to obtain the important post of Qadi of Seville, a remarkable prelude to his brilliant career as a jurist.)

(2) From 573/1177, during the transitional period in Andalusian intellectual life described above, his work entered a phase of doctrinal offensive. From this point onwards his expertise in the fundamentals of Law was coupled with study of the philosophy of practice, as found in the middle commentary on the *Nicomachean Ethics* of 1177.

For unknown reasons Ibn Rushd abandoned this path for a time and only returned to it in 591/1194 with his final commentary, the middle commentary on Plato's *Republic*. In the meantime he paid a visit to the court in Marrakesh (574/1178) and returned to Seville the following year to launch a personal doctrinal attack with his three most independent works: *Fasl al-maqal, Kashf 'an-manahij al-adilla* and *Tahafut al-tahafut*. This last was accompanied by other original philosophical works, namely the opuscules on the intellect which reconsidered and corrected the problematic of Ibn Bajja, and the *De substantia orbis*.

(3) Having seen this work endorsed by his appointment to the positions of Qadi of Cordoba and physician to the Sultan, Ibn Rushd devoted himself mainly to the large commentaries (*tafsir*). The first one on the *Posterior Analytics* seems to date from 576/1180. The final one on the soul was composed in 586/1190 and was extended in a special opuscule, *De animae beatitudine*. The commentaries themselves concentrate solely on the explanation of Aristotle's text. Where infrequently Ibn Rushd does differ with him or puts forward a personal opinion on a question Aristotle left unresolved, he is careful to indicate the fact.

The final part of his career was also taken up with reconsidering important 'questions', particularly in the field of logic, as well as with the completion of his medical and political work.

Thus after the logical and scientific preparation of the initial period, it was in the second phase that Ibn Rushd elaborated Averroism itself. In the third period he drew out the ultimate consequences of this approach, while trying to give as full a presentation as possible of the sphere of reason through in depth analysis of philosophy *par excellence* – namely Aristotelianism.

1

THE MAJOR OPTIONS

The following stages are known to have formed part of Ibn Rushd's first period of activity and enable us to reconstruct it with a reasonable degree of likelihood:

By his own account in *De caelo et mundo*, Ibn Rushd conducted astronomical observations during a stay in Marrakesh in 548/1153 at the age of twenty-seven.

His short commentary on the *Meteorology* is dated 554/1159. As this is the fourth in the collection of short commentaries on questions of physics, it is likely that the whole collection dates from the same period. From statements of doctrine found in the text it can also be deducted that the works of physics were preceded by the *Epitome of logic* (*al-daruri fi-l mantiq*) which would thus constitute the earliest of Ibn Rushd's written works, at least in the field of philosophy.

It should be noted that this Epitome was certainly not based on Aristotle's own text but follows al-Farabi and, to an extent, Ibn Sina. In general terms the 'short commentary' (*jami'*) or 'synopsis' is an independent work in which Ibn Rushd 'expounds the doctrine of Aristotle, adding, cutting out, seeking material in other works with which to complete the thought and introducing an order and method of his own' (Renan p.60). Consequently, M. Cruz Hernandez has pointed out that the usual term 'commentary' is inappropriate to these works, and he prefers to use the word 'readings' to indicate what there is in common in the different levels of Ibn Rushd's interpretation of Aristotle's text. While fully accepting this point, I propose here for the sake of convenience to continue using the usual term.

The middle commentary on the *Topics* is dated 563/1167, suggesting that this period concentrated upon the collection of works on logic and marked the start of the series of middle commentaries. In the 'middle commentary' (*talkhis*) Ibn Rushd hides behind Aristotle, following the order of his text and making frequent reference to it quoting only the first part of the passage in question. It requires the concerted efforts of scholars to pick out those passages where Ibn Rushd does introduce his own personal comments or examples drawn from his own civilization.

In 565/1169, working on the *De generatione animalium* and *De partibus animalium*, Ibn Rushd apologizes for the errors he may have made because, 'occupied with public affairs and being away from home' (he had recently been made Qadi of Seville), he was unable to check the texts. In fact, Ibn Rushd remained a jurist for more than ten years, before being appointed court physician. It is therefore very likely that it was around this time that he finished his major medical work *al-Kulliyat fi-l-tibb*, which mentions as already written the treatise *On Theriac* (which gave rise to a debate by letter with Ibn Tufayl), and also the commentary on Ibn Sina's didactic poem.

Other significant reference points include:

556/1170: middle commentary on the *De senso et sensato* and the *Parva naturalia* as well as the *Physics*.

567/1171: middle commentary on the *De caelo et mundo* written in Seville.

570/1174: middle commentary on the *Metaphysics* written in Cordoba.

The impression arising from this chronology is of someone initially feeling his way and trying out different avenues – medicine, astronomy, law – then taking as a guide the works of Aristotle as systematized since the time of Andronicus of Rhodes, and introducing a coherence into his approach by imposing a hierarchy upon his three offices: the first is a continuous work of commentary following the order of the system on different levels (i.e. short and then middle commentaries).

But this is not to say that he himself starts again from the beginning. In practice he allows the end of one series to overlap with the beginning of another, and the order of development is designed far more for the benefit of the reader than that of the commentator himself.

A theory can be put forward on this question. N. Morata has shown, using the *Taysir* of Ibn Zuhr, that the Almohad system had a special procedure to judge officially commissioned works. Ibn

THE MAJOR OPTIONS

Zuhr had to submit two versions of his work in order to get through this inspection. N. Morata suggests that the same must have been the case with Ibn Rushd's *Kulliyat* and this would explain the existence of two different versions, the second of which is only known through a Latin translation.

Perhaps this process could be generalized so that Ibn Rushd's undertaking of the middle and later the large commentaries could be attributed to his desire to comply better with the orders of the ruler. Since there is no break between the different levels, this may in fact represent an automatic reaction born of professional conscientiousness rather than submission to a formal critique expressed in hierarchical fashion.

The second office of Ibn Rushd is the practical work of a jurist, representing both his livelihood and his most important link with the Almohad system; and the third a medical work turned out on an occasional but fairly continuous basis which had the potential to lead on to a professional career should the opportunity arise.

This system, progressively introduced, helps us understand the different layers of richness in the work.

THE SCIENTIFIC OPTIONS

Although his astronomical observations constitute the first significant point in our chronology of Ibn Rushd, these should not be overrated.

His discovery from a mountain near Marrakesh of a previously unobserved star was simply the achievement of an enlightened amateur taking advantage of his comfortable financial circumstances and the various shifts of location necessitated by his career. It has little bearing on his own thinking which, by contrast, is strongly aprioristic.

Since the time of Ibn Bajja, there had been a certain amount of friction in Spain between the astronomers and the philosophers. This was not so much concerned with scientific competence in which the two groups were more or less equal though focusing on different fields. Nor was it due to a differing emphasis on the search for an all-embracing theory. Rather, the opposition was between a group of technicians who, accepting Ptolemy's explanatory scheme, limited themselves to perfecting it in mathematical terms and explaining it in depth, and on the other hand a group of thinkers accustomed to meditating upon hypotheses and principles.

While Ibn Bajja, as we shall see, is capable at times of coming up with new hypotheses, he and to an even greater extent the other philosophers are elsewhere subordinated to the rule of authoritative precedent rather than that of experience.

The criticisms against Ptolemy's system were levelled above all at his theory of the eccentric orbit of the spheres carrying the planets in relation to the Earth and the theory of epicycles designed to explain the apparent backward movement in the course of the stars. According to Aristotle all celestial bodies naturally and unavoidably move in circles. There must therefore be a non-celestial body that forms the central point around which this movement takes place – and this can only be the Earth.

Ibn Rushd adds to this principle a demonstration of the existence of four elements, thus implying that heavens are hollow in order to contain them. The idea of an 'enveloping sphere' centred on the Earth which would enclose the eccentric spheres and the epicycles is too obviously artificial to reconcile the Ptolemaic system with the Aristotelian vision.

According to Ibn Maymun (Maimonides) it was Ibn Bajja who first attacked the theory of epicycles in a text which has now been lost. He bases his argument on three principles drawn from Aristotle's *Physics*: the necessary existence of a fixed centre to all celestial movement, which can only be the immobile Earth; the need for this central point to be also the centre of the world; a sphere carrying the planets can only turn on its own axis and cannot move in epicyclic fashion. Ibn Bajja would have attempted to explain the observed difficulties purely in terms of the play of the eccentric spheres. However, his successors were to consider this hypothesis totally opposed to Aristotelian principles.

Ibn Tufayl in his turn condemned the theory of eccentric spheres. Though he did not produce a work of astronomy, he did formulate principles where were taken up on the one hand by Ibn Rushd, and on the other by the mathematician al-Bitruji.

Exiled in Egypt and working independently of these two but on a common ideological basis shaped by Almohadism, the Andalusian Jewish thinker Ibn Maymun also strove to overcome the contradictions of Ibn Bajja. Using a certain set of calculations he showed that the centre of the eccentric orbit of the various planets

THE MAJOR OPTIONS

was situated beyond the lunar sphere which was a relatively fixed section of the universe, and was therefore in the middle of the moving spheres.

But beyond this his analysis was purely philosophical, and he did not elaborate a scientific theory with which to back it up. He simply remarks in the *Guide of the Perplexed* that the ancients had not envisaged the idea that if the spheres carrying the planets had their axes inclined on the plane of the ecliptic and that of the equator of the fixed stars, this would make certain movements appear to take place – longitudinal, declining or the apparent variations in the arc described on the circle of the horizon by the heavenly bodies as they rise and set. But this still fails to explain the phenomena which underpin the theory of epicycles and eccentric spheres, namely the variations in speed and backward movement of the planets.

Ibn Rushd's progression is more complex. Though not himself an astronomer, he started off by making amateur observations of the heavens during his first two official visits to Marrakesh in order to take advantage of the clear skies of the region and observe stars not visible from al-Andalus, and also to compare observations of the same object from two distant places. Where there are disagreements in the commentators' understanding of Aristotle's text, Ibn Rushd also recommends observation in order to identify Aristotle's exact meaning. It is thus that he rejects the way in which Alexander of Aphrodisias conceived the Milky Way. Moreover, Ibn Rushd's short commentary of 554/1159 on *On The Heavens* is relatively independent of the original text – not just because, as mentioned, he adheres only to the basic structure, sometimes changing the order of exposition, but also because he goes on to demonstrations which differ from those of Aristotle, and are less rigorous.

However, his own experimental discoveries are not incorporated into this new arrangement and, in the field of cosmology at least, Ibn Rushd later discontinued his observations which had been made increasingly difficult by his overwhelming duties. At this point he moved closer to Aristotle's text attempting to give it the appearance of a proof, which is not necessarily the case.

In his middle commentary written in Seville in 567/1171, Ibn Rushd first of all divides the work into separate propositions, distinguishing the hypotheses from the conclusions, and reorganizing them into a triple refutation which is absent from the original text. The large commentary, written around 584/1188, takes this syllogistic organization right down to the level of textual detail, ending up on occasions with a partial result which goes beyond and even contradicts that of the author. Nevertheless, the work as a whole is far closer to the spirit of Aristotle than the short commentary.

The reason for this is Ibn Rushd's increasing emphasis on demonstration which leads him to draw more and more on other themes from Aristotle's work – in other words, giving precedence to 'the system' and even creating it artificially.

In the course of this development Ibn Rushd reconsiders his position, recognising that despite his youthful aspirations to become the individual who would revolutionize the field of astronomy, henceforth he could only set out the principles. He points out that the invention of epicyles (by Apollonius of Perga in the third century B.C.) occurred after Aristotle's time and was only endorsed by Ptolemy because of its greater simplicity. But for him it was still only a very convenient symbol and the main question was whether the mechanism it described was in fact possible. It was necessary to replace the geometric representation of the structure and movements of the universe with an exact depiction of reality.

According to Ibn Rushd, it must be possible to explain all heavenly phenomena, in particular the apparent variations in speed, by the hypothesis of movement in helix (*lawlab*) of which Aristotle speaks on several occasions. But Aristotle gave very little further explanation on this point and Ibn Rushd was reduced to making the somewhat tentative suggestion that this consisted of the movement of the pole of one sphere around the polar axis of another sphere. In any case, the helicoidal movement is visible for example in the daily movement throughout the year.

The mathematical model for this hypothesis was later provided by al-Bitruji (Alpetragius). It differs from Ibn Rushd's solely in that Ibn Rushd only accepts the existence of eight spheres, whereas al-Bitruji envisages a ninth situated above the sphere of the fixed stars and itself empty of stars and merely causing the movement of the other spheres. This movement is transmitted differently according to the distance from the enveloping sphere, and this explains the apparent accelerations and decelerations of simultaneously observed points. In addition, the poles of the different spheres do not coincide with the corresponding pole of the enveloping sphere, producing a difference between the ecliptic of

THE MAJOR OPTIONS

the fixed stars and that of the eighth sphere – hence the helicoidal movement (*haraka lawlabiyya*) or in snail shape (*haraka halazuni*) described by Ibn Rushd.

Once again, this model remained purely schematic and al-Bitruji limited himself to presenting what he had conceived not through observation but through 'a sort of divine inspiration',[1] recognising that he could not mathematically reconstruct the entire star system on this new basis. Despite this, the work was translated, starting in 1217, by Michael Scot, astrologer to Frederick II of Hohenstaufen and also translator of Ibn Rushd's large commentary on *On The Heavens*.

Until the sixteenth century the hypothesis of helicoidal movement was set in opposition to the Ptolemaic system enabling a resurgence of Aristotelian Physics (William of Auvergne, Robert Grosseteste) at a time when criticisms against it were mounting.

The effects of this were not wholly negative since al-Bitruji's work also echoed, this time in contradiction to Ibn Rushd, Ibn Bajja's ideas on dynamics. This leads us on to a second characteristic of Ibn Rushd's scientific explorations – that he shows very clearly the diversity of possible reactions to Aristotelian thought.

In a letter to his friend the converted Jew Yusuf Ibn Hasday, who had settled in Egypt and was author of a work on logic, Ibn Bajja gives an account of his intellectual development. In his native town of Saragossa he studied mainly music, and at that time the progression to astronomy was entirely natural. However, once he arrived in Seville, he realized the shortcomings of established astronomy. At the same time he was looking into certain questions of al-Farabi on the subject of demonstration. These two factors led him to launch into the study of Aristotle's *Physics*:

> Then I devoted myself to speculations on the *Physics*. I did not undertake this in order to work on what is clear in the *Akroasis Physike*. I undertook it because this work contains the principles, and all that comes after is derived from them. In particular, I focused on two very obscure questions.[2]

These concerned the indivisibles and the definition of the prime mover. With regard to the latter, Ibn Bajja points out that the eighth book of the *Physics* views the mover as wholly devoid of movement, while the seventh speaks of bodies that can be moved, but are called prime movers because they can cause movement without moving themselves. In his notes on the text of Aristotle itself, he reconsiders the notion of force (*quwwa*) and its relationship with movement, pointing out the ambiguity of the word *dynamis* which Aristotle uses to signify both a passive force (as opposed to the act) and an active force which produces movement. He comments that if a body causes another body to move, then the latter exerts an action on the mover, causing it fatigue (*kalal*). Thus without renouncing the concepts of agent and patient, he introduces that of active force, enabling quantity to be considered with regard to two forces of the same nature. Movement does not occur unless the action exceeds the reaction.

While claiming to give the true meaning of the work he is examining, Ibn Bajja in fact goes against its spirit. Despite his admiration for Ibn Bajja, Ibn Rushd reproaches him for this and elaborates a theory on the role of the surroundings on the simple movements of the sub-lunar bodies specifically in order to reject that of Ibn Bajja and return to Aristotle himself. He nevertheless borrows from him the idea that movement comes from an excess of motor force over the body that is moved, and he makes use of this to determine the speed of that movement.

It is only in the medical field that one can really speak of Ibn Rushd's scientific work, though even that remains on a philosophico-scientific level. A comparison of his medical works with his activities as an astronomer clearly shows where his true interests lay. As an astronomer he is little more than an amateur who was only able to carry out observations during his youth, whereas in medicine he is a specialist who remained devoted to the subject more or less throughout his life.

In his old age he was involved in writing middle commentaries in both fields – on Aristotle in the one, and mainly on Galen in the other, though at times emphasising his agreement with Aristotle (for example, regarding the generation of the blood). In his youth, on the other hand, there was an overall bias in favour of medicine in the production of treatises. Only one short commentary was given over to cosmology, whereas already his greatest work in this area was on medicine. Moreover, his continuous involvement in this field is clearly shown by the publication of his middle commentary on Galen's *On Fevers* in 589/ 1193 and the new version of *Kulliyat* the following year.

The Arabic and Latin versions that are known of this work are noticeably different both on specific points and in their overall

46

THE MAJOR OPTIONS

development. Only the Latin version contains a prologue attributing the commissioning of the work to the Sultan. The Arabic version, on the other hand, has an epilogue by the medical historian Ibn Abi Usaybi'a, who insists on Ibn Rushd's links with his colleague Ibn Zuhr.

A characteristic of medicine in al-Andalus, and doubtless what made it so successful, was that far from instigating a split as occurred in the field of astronomy where, as we have seen, the younger generation stood in opposition to the ancients' tradition of calculation, in medicine the scholars formed themselves into teaching groups far better organized than in the past. If there is a general tendency for the medical profession to run in families, this 'dynastic' phenomenon became even more pronounced. The most famous example is the Banu Zuhr who practised medicine through five generations. The most outstanding members were Abu-l-Ala (d.525/1130) and his son Abu Marwan (c.484/1091–558/1162) who was the most famous, and known in the Latin West as Avenzoar.

Ibn Rushd was on very good terms with Avenzoar and the epilogue of *Kulliyat* recommends as an option after this general work that the reader goes on to the *Kitab al-Taysir* ('Practical manual of treatments and diets') by his friend. This work, written between 515/1121 and 557/1161 was translated into Latin by John of Padua towards the end of the third quarter of the thirteenth century, and notably by Paravicini in 1281 under the title *Theicrisi da halmodana vahaltadabir*. Written at the order of the Almohad caliph, its purpose was to counteract the errors found in the practical manuals known at the time. While he follows his father in expounding the principle that experience is the only true guide, Ibn Zuhr in fact goes on to produce an essay designed to adapt observation to the established theoretical frameworks of the time. These came directly from Galen and consisted of the theory of the four elements of the macrocosm which correspond to the four humours of the human microcosm. Medicine works on allopathic principles and aims to rectify an excess of one or other of the humours, the criterion of heat and cold remaining in the body under treatment and not being absolute. In general, medicines are complex formulae containing a mixture of several ingredients which can substitute for one another, so that if one fails to take effect because of an idiosyncrasy in the patient, the other ingredients will have the same curative effect. The theory does not therefore go beyond a convenient means of arranging the subject matter – intuition and clinical observation continue to play a greater role. But the desire to organize knowledge in a scholar who was first and foremost a practitioner is nevertheless remarkable.

However, to understand Ibn Rushd's desire to systematize, it may be necessary to look to his mentors rather than his friend. In his biography we have seen the role that, according to Ibn Abi Usaybi'a and all the historians after him, was played by Abu Ja'far Ibn Harun de Trujillo (al-Trujali). To this should probably be added the influence through Ibn Jurayyul – who Ibn al-Abbar presents as a mentor of Ibn Rushd – of Ibn Jurayyul's own mentor, the famous Abu-l-Mutarrif Ibn Wafid (c.398/1007–467/1074). He is known above all for his work on agronomy, though this forms part of a whole corpus. The development of his works is important and in his 'general survey' (*Majmu'*) on agriculture, he frequently quotes classical and Eastern writers, albeit very few, and sometimes refers in a general way to the 'scholars'. His order of exposition is far more systematic than that of the Latin agronomists. His work is a practical manual filled with numerous details, sometimes picturesque, but none of which refer to the personal experiences of the author. It is, however, known from the biographer that he practised acclimatization and possibly artificial fertilization of plants. He was also the first person to study plants for themselves, and not for pharmacological ends. Although he was a physician, he separates the two fields, and while other authors talk at length in their agricultural treatises of the therapeutic applications of plants, he keeps this for another work. Moreover, his experience was more as a botanist than as an agriculturalist. As a result he is a balanced author. In a major work on simple drugs, he gathered a vast amount of bibliographical documentation while at the same time displaying great practical knowledge of certain remedies from his native region of Toledo. It is therefore not surprising that it should have been taken up and completed by Ibn Bajja in his *Book of Experiments* which has now been lost.

It is clear that Ibn Rushd's work forms part of a whole movement. By translating the Arabic *Kulliyat* (*Generalities*) by the Latin homophone *Colliget*, the medieval translator wished to emphasise the idea of a 'summary' incorporating the medical knowledge of the East as well as that of the West. While the work of Ibn Rushd is much shorter than Ibn Sina's great work *Canon of Medicine* (*Qanun fi-l-tibb*), which was brought to Spain in the time

THE MAJOR OPTIONS

of Abu-l-Ala b. Zuhr, it nevertheless incorporated the main substance of this work, taking into consideration the corrections made in particular by the Banu Zuhr. Moveover, this was the goal set by the Sultan who commissioned the work from Ibn Rushd – i.e. to subject all the different opinions in the field to a process of rational analysis and to make a collection of all those which turned out to be useful. Ibn Rushd for his part aimed to organize the material so as to produce a *compendium* of the art of medicine which would form a vital basis of knowledge acting as a springboard for more detailed investigations, and an aide-mémoire for those already versed in the subject. In dealing with semiology (Book IV) – which assumes lengthy experience – he apologizes for not going into greater detail while firmly pointing out that the work is addressed to members of the medical profession and that its aim is to synthesize.

The unique aspect of the work lies in the hierarchical status he accords to the 'generalities'. Aristotle stated that true science is the science of the universal. In the field of medicine the general truths lie beyond those gathered by observation, in the linking up of phenomena with their causes: hence his clearly stated claim to take Aristotle's *Physics* as his model, since it deals with the most general of subjects, providing basic principles from which more detailed matters can be broached. When he began the work, Ibn Rushd intended to follow it up with a second volume dealing with specific points. In the end he chose a different solution and finished his book by referring back to the *Taysir* of his friend, then during the course of his career picking up certain points in the different treatises, using Galen as his principal guide.

With the exception of anatomy, which was set apart due to its empirical nature (Book I), Ibn Rushd deliberately writes the rest of his treatise in 'a new language, unknown to the doctors of Antiquity and their predecessors, with demonstrations founded in natural philosophy' (prologue, beginning para.2). Thus from the start he avoided leaving the reader 'unable to reach the end of the book or even understand the greater part of it without a knowledge of logic sufficient at least to give him a grasp of the three forms of reasoning' (para.1). For example, the parameters allowing him to elaborate anatomical questions remained undefined because they were in fact none other than the Aristotelian categories – quality, quantity and so forth. At times Ibn Rushd even insists that more than in the works of Galen – who himself considered that the best kind of doctor was in equal measure a philosopher – he advocated the need to 'adopt something more of the philosophers' methods than those of physicians'. In this way he rejects amongst other things the theory of the great Greek physician according to which the movement of the muscle originates in the nerve. Ibn Rushd breaks down his argument into a syllogism and demonstrates that its form is incorrect, even before its premises come to be considered.

Without going so far as to say that theory is self-sufficient without proof by cure, Ibn Rushd challenges the kind of medicine which is centred entirely on results:

> We define medicine as the art which, starting from true principles, aims to preserve the health of the human body and to cure it of illness as far as is possible in a particular body. The aim of the art is not to effect an absolute cure but to do what can be done in so far as is possible at a given time. The results must then be awaited, just as in the art of navigation or war. (. . . .) Medicine has a theoretical side which forms part of natural science, and a practical side. The practical side is the experimental art of treatment and also the art of anatomy. But theory also plays a considerable role in considerations of health and sickness, above all those related to distant factors such as the elements and such like. With regard to the art of experimental medicine, this may teach one to recognise the powers of numerous remedies. But what we can understand by means of experiment is paltry compared to what it is necessary to know. Hence reasoning is vital as a means of explaining the causes of what we discover through experimental medicine. . . .
>
> (*Colliget*, Book I, para. 1)

A methodological significance should not therefore be attributed to terms such as study 'by the use of the senses' (*bi-l-hiss*) or 'lengthy observation' (*tul al-nazar*) or 'outward symptoms' (*zahara*) as if we were dealing with the description of a dissection. According to Aristotelian rules, the particular is the concern of the senses whereas the universal falls into the province of reason. The terms used by Ibn Rushd are no more than standard formulae indicating his level of thought, and not a call for experimentation. Thus, for example, he states that the spirit 'cannot be observed' in the liver, but can be 'observed' in the heart and the brain (Book I, para. 4).

THE MAJOR OPTIONS

Treatment in particular is founded on an inductive approach based on observing the effects of medicines – an approach which does not go beyond the level of generalization and differs from true medical science, which is based upon the study of causes and is deductive and demonstrative. Hence the scholastic method triumphs, i.e. formulation of the thesis, statement of the question, opinions and arguments.

Within this self-imposed strait-jacket, Ibn Rushd nevertheless managed to preserve a degree of freedom. He draws on various sources (although Al-Razi is by far the most important in anatomy), and his quotations are never servile; he allows himself to change the order of exposition, the vocabulary, and sometimes even to make a correction. But his choices are determined more by logical than by experimental criteria, above all in the enumerations. The most striking example is his long polemic, which concludes Book V, on the subject of mixing 'hot' and 'cold' medicines and the 'degree' of these qualities. Ibn Rushd savagely attacks Al-Kindi, himself a philosopher and doctor, who had drawn on mathematics and music to develop his theory of geometric proportions:

sensation		1	2	3	4	
medicine	1	2	4	8	16	

Ibn Rushd rejects this theory which was upheld in the nineteenth century by Weber and Fechner, preferring instead an arithmetic progression. But it is very strange that he chooses this by drawing upon arithmetic and musical bases similar to those of Al-Kindi. Yet he challenges Al-Kindi by invoking an empirical argument and asking how an organism could tolerate a medicine with a degree of sixteen.

Moreover, Ibn Rushd and his contemporaries did not succeed in perpetuating the most specific part of the Andalusian medical legacy as represented by the surgery of Abu-l-Qasim (Abulcasis) al-Zahrawi (fourth/tenth century) which constituted the best possible vehicle for experimentation. When discussing skull fractures, where splinters have entered the brain, Ibn Rushd declares it necessary to remove the bone around the wound, but then goes on to say without a trace of regret: 'But there is no one amongst us who knows how to carry this out' (Book VII, para.36). In his discussion of anatomy, Ibn Rushd's vocabulary occasionally betrays a desire to adopt a particular standpoint differing from that of his

51

predecessors. Yet their opinion is still upheld a little later in a discussion of the same subject. Such is the case, for example, with the cerebral nerves which Ibn Rushd initially says are 'joined' (*ittasala*) to the brain – static vision – then later adopts Al-Razi's expression according to which they 'extend from' (*kharaja*) it – dynamic vision.

Ibn Rushd's Aristotelianism often leads him to adopt a perspective different from that almost universally accepted since Galen. In his anatomical examination of compound members, he follows the principle of the three powers (natural, vital and animal), but does not introduce them in the traditionally accepted order. Elsewhere, he adopts an intermediate position between Aristotle and Galen. Aristotle classified the three powers as vegetative, sensitive and intellective, while Galen fused the intellective and sensitive into a single animal or psychic power and divided the vegetative into natural and vital. Ibn Rushd for his part identifies two essential powers: nutritive (corresponding to Aristotle's vegetative) and animal (corresponding, as was the case with Galen, to Aristotle's sensitive and intellective). Similarly he accepts the doctrine of the four humours but not the idea that the principles of genetics depend on their mixture. He prefers notions of cause (material, formal, efficient and final) and of the elements. He even demotes certain humours to the status of 'residues' on a par with urine. Only the blood and to an extent phlegm retain their traditional status.

However, in the science of Ibn Rushd, Aristotelianism remains more a method than a doctrine. Though he may rigidify rules which are considerably more subtle as conceived by Aristotle, he does not rely totally upon him in opposition to Galen. At times he even contradicts him. Such is the case in embryology where Aristotle defends the doctrine of *epigenesis* (that the germ is not composed of heterogeneous parts, but encloses them in potential form), and supports the theory of preformationism or *ontogenesis* of Hippocrates followed also by Albertus Magnus.

On the other hand, Galen's influence dominates in Ibn Rushd's functionalist vision. Where there is complexity of structure it is function that determines classification. Hence veins and arteries are distinguished only by the kind of blood they carry and not by their physical composition. Function represents the realization of potentialities, and it is these which form the subject of study in Book II (on health). The detailed study of muscles is kept for Book

THE MAJOR OPTIONS

II because, having mentioned their total number as 529, Ibn Rushd sees no reason to describe them in detail other than in terms of their finality – which in his view precludes the need for a specifically anatomical study.

The systematization which he pursues gives this work a particular status. Unlike his works of cosmology, it does not represent a somewhat servile return to an artificially rigid Aristotelianism built up into a formal system. Instead, it integrates a large part – though not all – of the medical teachings proved and tested over the years. But these 'proofs' are nevertheless still based on rational analysis which Almohadism had elevated to the level of universal touchstone, at least for the elite. This method places Ibn Rushd's medicine in the category of 'scholastic medicine'. This is well illustrated by his approach to anatomy. For the first time this is distinguished from physiology, but at the same time differs from the anatomy of Galen, who describes an animal in its vital movement, and that of Vesalius who at the time of the Renaissance would only admit the existence of a structure in man. His is the anatomy of 'the rationalized animal of Antiquity' (F. Rodriguez Molero), with a considerable effort to distinguish the organ from its function – though not in order to concentrate on its form, the function retaining a teleological value with regard to the constitution of the organ.

Despite its consequent weaknesses, Ibn Rushd's quest for absolute rationalization is not wholly sterile. He pushes to its ultimate limit the ideal of systematic knowledge accepted by his followers, and does not have to break with it, contradicting only specific theories. The notion that it was possible to grasp through the use of reason the whole of human existence down to its most everyday aspects was widespread at the time. It can be seen in latent form in works of primarily practical purpose, for example in recipe books which do not hesitate to stray into the realm of dietetics, and considerations of what is best *per se* for the health, leaving aside the influence of the passions. The idea is most consciously expressed in Ibn Tufayl's *Hayy ibn-Yaqzan*. First of all he examines the question of the emergence of living creatures, of the soul and thought, which correspond respectively to the birth of the hero on a desert island, his upbringing and his early experiences. The author has then only to set forth Aristotelian science in its own logical terms, before discussing the doctrine of the soul and that of God.

53

But a repercussion of the literary fiction of genetic analysis is that it provides indisputable evidence for the scientific theories invoked: all knowledge, medical, physical and cosmological, is arranged according to the necessary order governing all aspects of life. It is a paradox characteristic of this scientific doctrine that while refusing the empirical in the name of the necessary, its advocates feel the need to provide it with concrete underpinning.

In the *Kulliyat* Ibn Rushd goes even further along this path, and does not limit himself to founding his thought in the necessities of existence. In his opinion, the four intellectual faculties reside in the heart in accordance with Aristotle's cardiocentrism, but in lieu of proper organs have certain 'spots' in the brain where they manifest themselves: the imaginative faculty in the anterior section, the cognitive in the middle, the conservative (continuous activity) and the reminiscent faculty (discontinuous activity) in the posterior section. Apart from this localization there is another material substratum which is the heat transported by the heart to the brain which enables it to function.

However, the discussion immediately moves on to the most spiritual of levels: imagination only comes into play after sensation and in response to a 'signal' picked up from the latter by the 'common sense'. However, the spiritualization of the image is equally determined by a division of the space which controls the sequence of movement from one faculty to another. As for the universal idea that the rational faculty attains by this movement, if it is external to the individual in whom it is only briefly actualized, its 'memory' will nevertheless remain deeply embedded in society or humanity.

This incarnation of order, which is completely opposed to a platonic system of ideas, has two consequences. One, of a medical nature, is that 'health' depends on the suitability of an organism to the ontological order of nature. The other, of a metaphysical nature, is the idea that the Divine is approached through the contemplation of incarnate rationality: 'the person who concerns himself with anatomy is strengthened in his belief in God.' By extension, on the moral level, man and nature are fused in the same teleological structure established by God. Hence, while the roots of science in the spontaneous development of Andalusian culture explain why it attracted such a significant audience in the sixth/twelfth century, its natural religious consequences explain the resistance it came up against.

THE MAJOR OPTIONS

METHODOLOGICAL CONSEQUENCES

M. Cruz Hernandez has pointed out the complete absence of practical philosophical works amongst Ibn Rushd's short commentaries. This cannot be explained simply in chronological terms by the suggestion that just as Ibn Rushd was about to tackle this area he was diverted by the new undertaking of the middle commentaries. In fact, several short commentaries (on the *De partibus animalium*, *De generatione animalium* and *Parva Naturalia*) were produced at the same time as the middle commentaries. Instead, M. Cruz Hernandez puts forward an intersting hypothesis based on the first reading of the *Rhetoric* (*Historia de la Filosofia Hispano-musulmana*, II, pp. 194–5). In it Ibn Rushd writes that for the common people ethical life is to be realized through the intermediate ideal of 'eudemony', i.e. common happiness, which stems from the attainment of concrete goods such as good health, the right to a family, friendship, possessions and a good reputation. It is through this 'goodness' that well-being and happiness are achieved, and the implication seems to be that those inexperienced in the pursuit of wisdom have yet to reach the stage from which they can aspire to the intellectual ideal of the sage. The eudemony treated in the first reading of the *Rhetoric* therefore completes its logical and epistemological aspects and the group of short commentaries thus constitute a complete propaedeutic.

The first principle governing Ibn Rushd's work seems to be what might now be called the principle of completeness – in other words the need for an exhaustive approach. From this springs not only his enthusiasm for Aristotle, but also for the scholastic form of the commentary. Renan has already indicated the texts in which Ibn Rushd's devotion to Aristotle is most evident. The main idea to be found in them is that Aristotle alone managed to cover the entire field of human thought, and this is summed up in the statement that 'Aristotle's thought is the sovereign truth because his intelligence represents the limits of human intelligence'.

But we should not cling to this simplistic viewpoint, expressed all too often since the time of Ibn Sab'in in the seventh/thirteenth century. In practice, the statement has its counter. For example, in the short commentary on the *De Anima* the work begins with a statement of adherence to Aristotle as Ibn Rushd announces his intention to study only those areas on which the other commentators agree and which conform most closely with the

55

spirit of Aristotle. But immediately afterwards, he feels the need to clarify certain presuppositions which, he admits, are not found in the work he is considering but are nevertheless necessary in order to understand its thought. Some of these presuppositions are axioms drawn from other parts of Aristotle's work: every being that is generable and corruptible is composed of matter and form; matter has no essence; its only property is to be a state of potential; but it cannot be formless because otherwise it would be at once active, by hypothesis, and not active because it has no form; and so on. But other principles suppose a complex physico-medical theory: the principal composites of matter and form are the four simple elements, then bodies made up of a mixture of these four; the ultimate cause of their fusion lies in the heavenly bodies and the proximate cause is natural heat; next come the 'motor organs', heart, liver and so forth which make up the bodies of perfect animals; these motor organs cannot function without being informed by a soul; the proximate subject of this is heat, and therefore souls are one with regard to heat and multiple with regard to the faculties; the faculties are substances in the nutritive heat.

It is not only because he manages to integrate sixteen centuries of physico-medical thought that Ibn Rushd goes beyond simple exposition. As a doctor, he is able to distance himself from Aristotle's essentially biological conception of the question of the soul. Aristotle wished to make this question the introduction to the section of the *Physics* dealing with animate matter. He had therefore remained very vague on questions such as the rational faculty. He had previously made mention of this because logic led him to do so, just as having posed the existence of an intellect, which incidentally he defined as 'passive', his whole system led him to add to it another aspect of the intellect on which he does expand in *De Anima*, and which he does not even qualify — the term 'agent' only being introduced by the commentators.

Ibn Rushd on the other hand considers the problem so closely that in this short commentary alone he elaborates two theories of understanding. The first is influenced by Ibn Bajja: according to this theory, the universals to which the understanding aspires do not exist outside the soul as do things sensible, but depend upon the individual imagination and hence differ as do individuals. Aristotle did not therefore reason in the same way as an uneducated man. Material perception is therefore the readiness of the

THE MAJOR OPTIONS

imaginative forms to receive intelligibles. Ibn Rushd faithfully records this early opinion held in his youth, and later corrects it: if understanding were fused with the material aspects of the imagination, it could no longer receive separate intelligences.

The preceding description is therefore only valid for the common herd who always remain on an inferior level of intellection. Their intelligibles are confined to the practical, generable and corruptible. The educated man on the other hand rises to the level of speculative intelligibles, first those which require a training and depend on the imagination, then those of physics which also rely on it, and finally those which exist in themselves and which could be considered metaphysical and are eternal. Hence the formula found in the Sunna: 'Know your essence and you will know your creator.' Man, who is the great wonder of the universe, is an intermediary between God and nature – at once corruptible and eternal. The state of ultimate perfection, according to Ibn Rushd, is the same as that to which the Sufis aspire, but they cannot attain it by their methods since in order to do so, it is necessary to go through all the stages of speculative science. The only correct part of their thinking is that at this level the senses cease to play a part and all the other faculties of the soul are absorbed into the understanding. The universality which the soul possesses to a certain degree is neither that of the higher intelligibles and even less that of God. There are various degrees of universality which explain the continued existence of a certain multiplicity in their separate substances.

This example demonstrates the complexity of the mental universe within which Ibn Rushd moved. For him, Aristotle's thought was not simply what is given in the texts, but everything that is coherent with them once they have been correctly interpreted. On this point Ibn Rushd is in complete agreement with all the *Falsafa* who had never been concerned with philosophical *problems* as such, but rather with the *cultural system* built on philosophy. The only difference is that he considers this system to be incarnated in the work of Aristotle *alone*, and faithful to the rationalist, anti-mystical ideals of Almohadism, he makes the assumption – justified in retrospect, but risky in terms of the resources of information available at the time – that the work had been distorted.

Hence his criticisms of Ibn Sina. Beyond certain technical points (the distinction of the possible and the necessary, procession from

57

the One, etc.) it is Ibn Sina's mystical approach that he opposes — his confusion of the data of physics and metaphysics (introduction of the proof of the Prime Mover into the field of metaphysics), confusion of the transcendental and the material (with regard to the problem of unity), acceptance of the immediate action of the separate forms on the world of generation, attribution of an imaginative faculty to the heavenly bodies, etc. In other words, Ibn Sina did not respect the natural division of such questions and mixed philosophical analysis with incompatible metaphysical notions. As R. Arnaldez comments:

> unlike Avicenna who strives to deduce, at least theoretically, the physical from the metaphysical, Averroes is essentially a philosopher of nature. In a passage of commentary on Book Λ of the *Metaphysics*, he writes, in express opposition to Avicenna, that unless the metaphysician instantly requested (*yusadiru*) of the physician that he pass on to him the idea and the reality of movement, he would have no knowledge of it. Physics is therefore fundamental, and metaphysics simply crowns the whole structure of the positive sciences.[3]

These criticisms also had a formal consequence: while the style of the middle commentaries is strongly reminiscent of the oriental model, Ibn Rushd denies himself any recourse to their rhetorical style (arresting titles, encyclopedic developments, etc.).

These principles of completeness and coherence culminate in Ibn Rushd's discovery of the method of internal criticism of a text under commentary. The idea, which now seems so commonplace, that a certain author 'might', or 'might not' have said a certain thing, was a great novelty in the milieu with which we are dealing. One has only to think of the vast syncretism between Aristotelianism and neoplatonism that arose simply out of the historical accident by which fragments of Plotin were handed down under the title of 'Theology of Aristotle'. Al-Farabi's work on the agreement between Plato and Aristotle shows the extent to which great thinkers could be led astray in this way.

Ibn Rushd spontaneously employs techniques of internal criticism, impressing modern experts with his penetrating intuitions. Not only does he reject all neoplatonic contaminations, but he is also capable in many places of correcting the faulty translations from which he was forced to work. It has even been suggested that he had some knowledge of Greek but, as A. Badawi has demonstrated, his approach incorporates three different methods of textual criticism (*Multiple Averroes*: pp. 59–89). First, he compares the different translations available to him, since he is specific in attributing his quotations to different 'copies' of the work. Second, he indicates the lacunae in the text he is using, which may have been marked by the translator himself and which he sometimes completes, either by referring to another translation, or sometimes even on his own authority based on his knowledge of Aristotle. It is this last technique that allows him to go beyond a purely philological approach and which leads on to the final method by which he sometimes judges that the text before him is incoherent or absurd and with considerable judgement puts forward an alternative reading. Finally, it should be pointed out that this is not a case of lengthy and creative discourses shaped by a predetermined and inflexible stance concerning the supposed perfection of the Great Master. For one thing, Ibn Rushd situates Aristotle within a sketch outlining the entire progress of human thought. Picking up an idea already found in Al-Kindi, Ibn Rushd praises the ancient philosophers who preceded Aristotle, saying that whatever Aristotle's own particular genius, he was nevertheless indebted to them for their part in his 'education' (*In Metaph.* 993 b.11). He also admits that progress can continue after Aristotle, if only on specific points, remarking on several occasions, 'as Aristotle would have intended . . . and in accordance with truth (or reason)'.

CULTURAL COMPLEMENTS

We can also find in the works of Ibn Rushd's early period complementary indications which reveal not only his scientific and philosophical outlook, but also his cultural viewpoint. For this we refer to two works dealing, not with natural science, but with specifically human questions. These are his two middle commentaries on the *Poetics* and the *Rhetoric* which, according to Renan, date from 570/1174

In the former, Ibn Rushd appears as a fairly typical representative of the class of Cordoban jurists, much given to versification (he produced several didactic poems), but impervious to major contemporary developments (such as the appearance of the *muwashshah* or strophic poetry on the one hand, and on the other the *zajal* written in dialect by writers such as Ibn Quzman who left several verses in praise of Ibn Rushd). This was in spite of the fact that the new forms had spread extremely rapidly throughout the Arab World.

In this work one continues to feel the reverberations of the fourth/tenth-century polemic between the advocates of ancient and modern poetry, and one comes across the old philological arguments employed by the followers of classicism (*mutaqaddimun*) against the calls of the modernists (*muhdathun*) for freedom of inspiration. Ibn Rushd's work is one of plain commentary rather than a work of doctrine, and does explicitly state his own position. However, over half the poetic quotations are taken from pre-Islamic or Ummayad writers, and of those 'modern' poets who are quoted most are writers such as Abu Tammam or Mutanabbi who continued to employ the traditional bedouin patterns and motifs within the new forms. The only true representative of the 'moderns' who is quoted is Ibn al-Mu'tazz, whose merit lay above all in the perfection of his language. Popular poetry is barely touched upon in passing.

This marked preference is all the more surprising in view of Ibn Rushd's declared intention to 'sum up the general laws found in Aristotle's *Poetics* that are common to all or the majority of peoples', and for this reason, he says, he will leave aside those parts which are only of relevance to Greek poetics. In the end, Ibn Rushd goes beyond the purely literary to give us a general sketch of his whole cultural milieu, as Aristotle had done for his. It is merely a sketch, because he relies on an ancient oriental translation of extremely poor quality where specific concepts are misunderstood, translated in several different ways or even completely distorted in cases where they deal with literary forms which do not exist in Arabic. Ibn Sina had already tried before him to produce a commentary on the work of Aristotle which was taken to be part of the *Organon*. He was aware that the artistic forms of the Greeks were specific to them as were those of the Arabs. But immediately after this opening remark he went straight on to an explanation of the former in terms of the latter, allowing himself to be directed by faulty translations while following Aristotle's text in fairly systematic fashion.

The merits of Ibn Rushd's work stand out by comparison. He is capable of avoiding the totally theoretical kind of paraphrase which lacks all connection with reality. Leaving aside those parts outside his grasp he follows the order which seems most appropriate,

THE MAJOR OPTIONS

drawing strongly on his own culture in an attempt to come up with a correct interpretation. But the conditions in which this work was carried out prevent it from having any value other than philosophical.

Still more worthy of note is the extension brought about by Ibn Rushd in the field of logic. While in his works of poetics he cannot help reducing the cultural to the philosophical, in logic on the other hand his philosophical technique has a direct bearing on his own life and milieu.

The development of logic in al-Andalus was totally dominated by al-Farabi once Ibn Hazm's attempt to expound the subject using terms from everyday life and from the law had been crushed. Even at the start of the seventh/thirteenth century the last of the great Spanish logicians, Ibn Tumlus of Alcira, who is assumed to have been a pupil of Ibn Rushd, still made no mention of Ibn Rushd's commentaries on the *Organon* while making prominent reference to al-Farabi. The current tendency was to emphasise the formal consequences while ignoring the basic philosophical problems. In this field, the main contribution of the Andalusian scholars was reduced to the particularly advanced formalization found in the *Compendium* of the scholar and musician Abu-l-Salt (b. Denia 460/1067 and living in Seville until he left Spain in 488/1095), which did not resurface in the West until two centuries later. Apart from this, his *Rectification of the Intellect (Taqwin al-dhihn)*[4] follows Aristotle to the letter apart from a few changes in the order of exposition and definitions where he supplies a fuller explanation or more developed extension than his model. When in the seventh/thirteenth century the mystical philosopher Ibn Sab'in of Murcia attempted to complete the Aristotelian legacy, he diverged from al-Farabi only in a few respects – all formal – borrowed from oriental writers (Brethren of Purity, Ibn Sina) and in particular by his introduction into the field of the logic of categories of the emanationist doctrine of the Muslim neoplatonists.

Ibn Rushd is the only writer to go beyond formalism without leaving aside the problems of expression. Although the *Rhetoric* was at the time universally considered to belong to the *Organon*, Ibn Rushd understood that Aristotle's intention in it was not so much argument as communication. Al-Farabi's influence is also present but in a similar way as in his works of political philosophy, and not as in the works of other Andalusian logicians. Rather than refer to his short commentary on the *Rhetoric*, which essentially relates to

Book I concentrating on the logical aspects (notably syllogism and rhetorical induction), Ibn Rushd draws on the large commentary which he uses, as with politics, to adapt the basic text to the context of Islamic culture. This is an indispensable work if one goes beyond the objective knowledge it contains to look at its subjective effects. In this way we return to the realm of politics, since rhetoric is addressed to others and not to oneself, to a group rather than an individual, is based on universally accepted views rather than personal feelings and pursues the practical goal of inciting people to action.

This commentary, contemporary with the propaganda efforts of the Almohad regime with its hierarchical arrangement of the forms of discourse, expresses the author's awareness that rhetorical language speaks to the human being as a whole and not merely his intellect, aiming to instil belief (*tasdiq*) which may correspond to the truth, but also to the plausible or even the false. The problem had already been posed implicitly in the Almohad *Profession of Faith* since, in Ibn Tumart's opinion, the truth of revelation depends upon the sincerity (*sidq*) of the Prophet but, if it is to be taken as true rather than just plausible, it nevertheless requires confirmation from God in the form of a miracle. Hence Ibn Rushd goes further than the text on which he is commenting in his analysis of the 'political lie' which a leader must use to deal with unsophisticated souls, and this is clearly distinguished from formulae couched in a deliberately mythological expression whose falsity is not plain, as is the case with the 'enigmas' (*alghaz*) of the 'politicians'. What later came to be parodied by the term 'double truth' originated in these diverse expressions of the truth, already issued by the Almohad Mahdi, in forms adapted to suit different levels of intellect.

Apart from their own intrinsic interest these studies, which were still considered to fall into the sphere of logic, enabled a fundamental difficulty put forward by the grammarians to be overcome. Since the introduction of Greek logic into the Muslim World, the grammarians had refused to mix the rules of logic with those of language. The general outline of this conflict can be traced in a famous debate which took place in fourth/tenth-century Baghdad between the Muslim scholar, al-Sirafi, and the Nestorian logician, Matta Ibn Yunus. Their arguments ranged over the incompatibility of the Hellenic and the Semitic categories, the difference between 'designation', particular to each language, and

THE MAJOR OPTIONS

the universal idea of 'name', problems associated with religion, since Arabic was the language of revelation, and so forth. To this was added the feeling expressed by the great prose writer Jahiz, when he described the Arabs as the 'masters of language' (*ahl al-lisan*). This feeling was particularly prominent in the anti-Christian polemics of al-Andalus, which were invariably reduced to showing that the enemy could not understand what he was discussing since it was only accessible to those who could grasp the subtleties of the Arabic language, the exact sense of its words, images, grammatical distinctions and so forth.

The question of the relationship between logic and grammar was also raised in Muslim Spain and though it revolved around a particular grammatical question rather than the subject in general, the discussion was equally detailed and comprehensive as in the East. In Saragossa at the beginning of the sixth/twelfth century, two of the great intellectual authorities of the time confronted each other in a series of debates. They were Ibn Bajja, a philosopher of the Aristotelian school, and Ibn al-Sid de Badajoz, who was primarily a grammarian and man of letters but also a thinker in the tradition of a neoplatonism diffused throughout the Muslim World and whose Hellenic roots had become blurred.

In one of the 'questions' raised, based on the exposition of a brief poetic text, Ibn al-Sid loftily affirms the independence of the disciplines, drawing particular distinction between the question of comprehension and that of coherence.

> In the art of grammar, expressions may sometimes be adequate, sometimes inadequate to express the meanings, provided the listener understands what the speaker is trying to convey. In the expression, something may be linked with a certain thing while pertaining to something else in terms of meaning, provided the interlocutor has recognised the intention of the speaker. The content of the mesage is identical in both cases.[5]

The approach of Ibn al-Sid and Ibn Tumart, though differing in both literary and religious terms, but nevertheless parallel, shaped the attitude of Ibn Rushd who was finally to express his agreement with the grammarian in opposition to the writer whom he nevertheless admired greatly. Or perhaps it could be said that he integrated into the field of philosophy that which had been rejected by the followers of an exaggerated formalism. The reason for this is that he was more sensitive than Ibn Bajja to the cultural foundations of thought and accepted that the phenomena he was examining were not, as Ibn al-Sid had already pointed out, 'a poetic necessity, but the plain talk of the Arabs as used in their everyday conversation'.[6]

INVOLVEMENT IN THE MUSLIM COMMUNITY

We have just seen undeniable evidence of Ibn Rushd's wish to integrate his thought and his environment into a single whole. As a result, one cannot ignore, even in a philosophical study, his activity as a *faqih* – i.e. as Almohad teaching insistently recalled, someone working within the civilization of Islam who excelled in producing a 'comprehensive' work.

The authenticity of Ibn Rushd's legal works has sometimes been called into question in view of the absence of characteristic references to the works of philosophy. It has also been suggested that the work *Bidayat al-Mujtahid wa nihayat al-Muqtasid* (translated by R. Brunschvig as 'The beginning for he who is striving – towards a personal judgement – and the end for he who contents himself – with received knowledge') could have been written by another member of the numerous Banu Rushd who were Qadis and at least three of whom had written works of Law. Yet the date of around 564/1168, which by chance is given in the work as the date of composition (with the chapter on the Pilgrimage added in 584/1188), does correspond with the chronology of the author known in the West as Averroes. This was in fact just before he was appointed Qadi of Seville, a very important post which the expertise displayed in the treatise would have justified. Moreover, the relatively watertight divisions between the different spheres of activity in a single author is not necessarily surprising since Muslim law was a field in itself. Prior to Ibn Rushd, Ibn Tumart, as mentioned, developed a purely rational theology on the one hand, and a wholly practical juridical methodology on the other. Even a Jewish author such as Ibn Maymun – whose intellectual formation had taken place in a milieu dominated by Almohadism – started out in his *Book of Elucidation* (*Kitab al-Siraj*) by adopting positions different from those he was later to defend during his exile in the East.

In particular, the rationalism which formed the basis of Ibn Rushd's work and of Almohadism itself is clearly discernible in the

THE MAJOR OPTIONS

Bidaya. The work is a treatise of *ikhtilaf,* in other words one designed to expound the solutions put forward by the various schools on each item of law. Essentially these consisted of the three great Sunni doctrines: Hanafi, Maliki and Shafi'i which were the oldest of the schools. In addition, Ibn Rushd frequently examined Hanbali and Zahiri teachings. On almost all occasions he quotes the opinions of the founders of the small early schools which may have been adopted by the great doctors or which were close to their thinking. He also refers to the ancient thinkers invoked as authorities, as well as to the divergences reported by tradition between doctors of the same school. Finally, on very rare occasions, Kharijite or Shi'ite solutions are indicated.

On the other hand, the work was also written for a personal and practical purpose as stated in the introduction, and coming from a country governed by Maliki law, the author shows himself especially familiar with the traditions of that school and its many finer points, to the extent that he envisages a future treatise on the particular questions *(furu')* arising within that tradition. The fact that he does not accord it any preference in his development of the work tallies with his intention, made clear from the beginning – to stick to the fundamental questions amenable to a general set of rules. There is no doubt that these fundamental questions are fixed upon in somewhat arbitrary fashion – some being considered as such on occasions and as *furu'* on others. Yet this arose from a desire for clarity evident in Ibn Rushd's approach, which respects the major traditional divisions in Muslim law while introducing a very detailed structure of sub-divisions particularly when the subject matter is too wide-ranging. In particular the explanation of the divergences is always accompanied by an account of their causes, sometimes brief and at other times more lengthy, in order to furnish objective 'proofs' for each opinion. If he does not know the proof invoked by the doctor in question, Ibn Rushd puts forward one that he considers most appropriate. Sometimes he even provides one he considers better than that which was in fact put forward. If, as happens most often, he cannot decide between the different solutions, it is not unusual for him to qualify the ideas put forward as 'weak' or even 'absurd'. Where he does have a preference, he bases this on his conception of what is 'better' or 'clearer'. As a rule, the work is dominated by the hierarchical arrangement of general principles and specific points, the former governing the latter and preceding them in the order of exposition.

65

In this, it is like his commentary on Plato's *Republic* and similar also to the approach he advocates with regard to medicine in the end of the *Kulliyat*.

The importance of the *Bidaya* lies in that 'it appears to represent the most advanced existing example of the methodical application of *Usul al-Fiqh* – both as hermeneutic and as a basic reference point – to the whole corpus of Sunni fiqh' (R. Brunschvig: 'Averroès juriste', pp.43–4). Ibn Rushd had many predecessors who had also undertaken to explain the divergences by studying the methods of deduction behind the various solutions using legal sources. A notable example was the Andalusian al-Baji in the fifth/eleventh century. But Ibn Rushd was the only one not to lapse into a polemic in favour of one school. The *Usul* (fundamentals) are outlined in the introduction which deals with the different methods of exegesis giving rise to divergences. Ibn Rushd's preferred source of reference is the traditions, particularly those of the Prophet validated by their inclusion in the great canonical compendia. Generally adopting an approach close to the Shafi'is in his treatment of these traditions, Ibn Rushd adopts Ibn Hamz's decisive stance, preferring the definite to the probable, thus parting company with Ibn Tumart who followed the Shafi'is. He differs from him also in not taking up a position on the question of the conclusive value of the different forms of the traditions. On the other hand, he does oppose the Maliki predilection for the Medinite practice, objecting that either one invokes a limited consensus (*ijma'a*) which proves nothing, or one invokes a prophetic usage transmitted through multiple channels and this needs to be supported by a saying of the Prophet. Thus he reduces the Medinite practice to the level of an additional criterion.

A consensus is only valid, according to Ibn Rushd, if supported by a text or a rational interpretation of a text, and it only serves to transform the probable into the obligatory. He accepts the use of reasoning by analogy because of the existence of unlimited concrete examples, whilst the basic texts and the Prophet's acts and silences of assent were much fewer. Like Ibn Hazm, he recognises that this form of reasoning did not appear until after the death of the generation of the Prophet's Companions, but does not for this reason consider it a reprehensible innovation (*bid'a*), because it is justified firstly in rational terms but also by the scriptures. However, this method only enables a progression from one particular to another, and analogy is in no way connected with syllogism although the same word (*qiyas*) is used to describe both. Nor can it override tradition, unless the tradition is imperfectly established. Where the two contradict each other, allegorical interpretation (*ta'wil*), beloved of Almohadism, can be applied.

While taking a stern view of Zahiri literalism, which he considers stultifying, he is attentive to the exact meaning of language as well as to logic. He deplores the servile imitation of his Maliki predecessors and advocates personal effort (*ijtihad*) particularly in considering the many questions difficult to reduce to rule, and as a general means of making an informed choice between the various solutions put forward by the different schools he is examining.

In his definition of the good jurist, Ibn Rushd adopts the example used by Aristotle in the *Sophistical Refutations*, describing a good cobbler as one able to produce a shoe exactly fitting the client, and not one offering numerous ready-made models. While Malik is sometimes criticised for his lack of logic on a specific point and at others praised as generally the most competent jurist, his recent disciples are most frequently denounced for their useless complications.

At once close to the spirit of Almohadism and distant from certain of its theses, Ibn Rushd's judicial work exemplifies the extent to which Spain was capable of adopting the doctrine of its new rulers. This remains very limited if one considers that although Ibn Rushd became the fourteenth most important Andalusian authority of his generation in terms of the audience he acquired (cf. *Le Monde des ulémas andalous*, p.178), he nevertheless remained isolated even during the process of doctrinal renewal following the establishment of the new rulers. In the next generation the division became even more acute with a majority following a syncretic approach much less rigorous than that of Ibn Rushd, standing in opposition to a minority mindlessly devoted to the new rulers.

Although at the time its influence did not extend beyond the personal sphere of action of the lone Qadi, Ibn Rushd, the conciliation effected in the *Bidaya* is nevertheless a milestone in the evolution of Muslim law as a whole. On the one hand, it prefigures the modern tendency to avoid adherence to a single school and to take into account the solutions put forward by other doctrines, and even by individual ancient authorities. On the other hand, the rationality built into its approach prepared the way for the new science of 'the finality of the law' (*Maqasid al-Shari'a*) of which the Andalusian founder, al-Shatibi (eighth/fourteenth century) opposed certainty to the conjectural character of traditional juridical methodology. The problem was to deduce from the Koran and the Sunna conceptual principles such as: 'No prejudice or harm', 'He has placed no constraint in religion' – the sole objective of religion being the interest (*maslaha*) of men in their lives and their relationship with God. Hence the general principles based on certainty must not only precede and govern the specific questions as was the case in Ibn Rushd, but there must be a dialectical relationship between the former which are categorical and the latter which are conjectural. Moreover, in both writers the juridical indications of absolute scope concerning everyday aspects of community life are reduced, in essence, to rational principles (justice, generosity and so forth), and the function of the religious precepts, which are not subject to speculation, is to reinforce them.

2

THE INTERPRETATION OF ALMOHADISM

In contrast to the eras of the emirate and the caliphate (which lasted until the end of the fourth/tenth century), the next two and a half centuries were largely times of crisis for Muslim Spain, despite episodes of considerable stability.

The fall of the caliphate at the beginning of the fifth/eleventh century ensured the sudden breakdown of the initial pattern of organization in the intellectual world of al-Andalus – a pattern that was both official but also spontaneous. Although the establishment of Almoravid rule did not bring important changes from this point of view in relation to the Taifa period, throughout this century and the beginning of the next there was an effort at restructuring along new geographical, social, political and cultural lines. As a result, there was a shift from a system of organization based on the complementarity of disciplines within a specifically Muslim system of education, to a hierarchy of spiritual authorities within the official doctrine of the Almoravids. The apogee exactly coincided with the end of the era of Almoravid political domination. Nevertheless the system was not strictly monolithic since there was still one current which, despite being integrated into the whole, diverged from the line taken by the majority. Within the latter, juridism which had previously dominated to a considerable extent and been developed for its own sake, was increasingly subordinated to a reforming effort leaning towards study of the prophetic Traditions, i.e. in conformity with the spirit of true Malikism. These specialists in the practice of the Law, who had considerable influence on the masses, can be distinguished from those specializing in the sacred Book who appear to have pursued disinterested research.

The next generation broke completely with this form of

organization, but only to a noticeable extent some twenty years at least after the political establishment of the Almohads – in other words the time taken for a generation of eminent masters to disappear. There were many fewer masters of significant influence, Ibn Rushd being the fourteenth in order of importance and the last of this group. Moreover, he was linked to the minority tendency of the preceding period rather than that of the majority. The conception was broader and more organic: the idea of complementarity was readopted from the Taifa period and that of multidisciplinary teaching by each master from the Almoravid era. There was also a desire to integrate new forms of thought: mysticism (Ibn al-Mujahid, founder of the Sevillian school, was the ninth master in order of importance), philosophy, in the case of Ibn Rushd who was also considered a jurist but not just one, and even the possibility of acquiring a moral authority as a specialist in the purely literary disciplines.

However, such an ambitious structure was hard to achieve and Ibn Rushd remained isolated in the midst of his group, despite the audience he acquired. Hence, from the next generation onwards there was a major regrouping based on a compromise, placing greater emphasis within the Andalusian tradition, as it had previously arisen, on disciplines such as *Kalam* and juridical methodology, while allowing Sufism to develop in a separate sphere, aligning itself outwardly with the rest of intellectual and political life, and suppressing the audience once gained by philosophy. The most striking new feature, representing a conservative reaction to the Christian threat, was the importance acquired by Qur'anic and Arabic studies.

Completely separate from this group, which made up a considerable majority, a very small circle strove to perpetuate the specific legacy of Almohadism, but without understanding its implications and breaking it down into already recognised elements – Zahirism and Ash'arism. It should be observed that this circle centred round one figure, Abu Muhammed ibn Hawt Allah, who, according to al-Ansari, claimed to be a pupil of Ibn Rushd but does not seem to have drawn on his philosophical teaching. He is known chiefly as a docile tool of the regime who was dispatched on missions to delicate areas, such as the Balearics after the expulsion of the last upholders of the Almoravid system. (On all this see *Le Monde des ulemas andalous*, pp.45–104 and 137–86.)

RUSHDIAN THEOLOGY

Amongst the works of Ibn Rushd *Kashf 'an manahij al-adilla* is clearly dated 575/1179–80 – i.e. during his second period as Qadi of Seville, henceforth capital of al-Andalus. The experts agree that *Fasl al-maqal* and *Tahafut al-tahafut* date from the same years. These three works together with the brief *Damima* are the only ones in which the author speaks solely for himself. They form an independent block between two large groups of commentaries, coming after all the brief commentaries and before all the large ones (or just as he was beginning the series). They also fall within the period of transformation in Andalusian intellectual history just described. During his first official posting to Seville in 565/1169 and then to Cordoba two years later, Ibn Rushd restricted his role to that of Qadi since the environment was not yet sufficiently favourable. During his second posting to Seville, however, he was able to profit from the major renewal of intellectual personnel taking place in order to launch his personal doctrinal offensive.

As we have seen, Ibn Tufayl relied on the Almohad doctrine which can be found in the account of the early stages of thought. Subsequently, however, he took advantage of a partisan confusion to graft on a completely alien outlook – that of illuminism. Ibn Rushd, meanwhile, adhered to rationalism and rejected all claims to transcend it, viewing the analysis of the sphere of reason as the loftiest of peaks.

There is a manuscript preserved in the Escorial (cited by Renan pp. 73 and 464) which includes a list of the works of al-Farabi, Ibn Sina and Ibn Rushd. Under the name of Ibn Rushd is mentioned a 'Commentary on the profession of faith of the imam and Mahdi (Ibn Tumart)' (*Sharh 'aqidat al-imam al-mahdi*). This work has not survived and this is the only reference to it. It would have been an interesting work in showing how Ibn Rushd dealt with the order of reasons set out in the thought of the Mahdi himself. Although it is generally considered a work of secondary importance, *Kashf 'an manahij al-adilla* ('Discovery of the methods of proofs') is useful in revealing how he took up almost all the Almohad theses without, however, explicitly referring to Ibn Tumart and following a completely different order for reasons that were doctrinal and above all pedagogic.

Proof of the existence of God was traditionally undertaken by stating the necessity of the existence of a creator. Like all the Muslim theologians, Ibn Tumart started from the Qur'anic verse

(XIV,11) affirming this necessity, but he differed from them in leaving out all reference to sensible experience and adhering to the 'necessity of reason'. This same rationalism recurs later in the demonstration of *Fasl al-maqal*, which suggests that it is the Qur'an itself that invites rational argumentation. This argument is taken up again in the *Kashf* against the literalists and the Sufis. However, Ibn Rushd adheres to it most closely in refuting the apologist-theologians *(mutakallimun)*, whose method was inaccessible to the masses but nevertheless did not constitute an apodictic demonstration.

In the analysis of the idea of creation, Ibn Rushd followed the same path as Ibn Tumart's *Profession of faith*, starting out from experience but refining it in such a way that the analysis revolved around ideas alone: a) experience of the existence of animate beings which bear witness to a Providence and are necessarily created; b) inference from the existence of created things of the existence of a Creator. However, Ibn Tumart focused on the mechanism of this inference itself, deducing from it a reversal of the analogy with regard to our experience of creation and positing God as the Perfect Being. Ibn Rushd, on the other hand, introduced a 'scientific' perspective at this point, affirming the necessity, in order to have exact knowledge of the existence of God, of possessing the knowledge of the substance of things. In this they diverged to the same extent as Descartes and Spinoza. The parallel can be taken even further, since Ibn Tumart immediately elaborated his profession of faith on the rational level and only subsequently provided simplified versions in his *murshidat*, whereas Ibn Rushd distinguished two kinds of knowledge from the same two proofs (through Providence and through the 'idea' of creation): that of the masses who could only understand them in terms of their sensible experience, and that of the intellectual elite who were capable of perceiving in them apodictic proofs.

This divergence obliged Ibn Rushd to write a special chapter – admittedly very short – in which he took up the problem of the unicity of God, using the same method and the same argument as before except for some new quotations from the Qur'an. He was forced to make this repetition because he failed to understand Ibn Tumart's logic which, by immediately insisting on the separation of creature and Creator, could immediately posit the Absolute Being.

In the chapter on the divine attributes, however, the *Kashf*, like

THE INTERPRETATION OF ALMOHADISM

the *Profession of faith*, turned straight to the Qur'an for its own sake and no longer simply to give content to a primarily rational argumentation. Ibn Tumart stated that

> the names of the Creator are subject to His authorization, He is not named except by that which He named Himself in His book, or by the words of His prophet. Analogy, etymology and convention are unlawful concerning these names.

He defined the attributes saying that 'God is necessarily living, knowing, powerful, endowed with a will, hearing, sight, speech and all this without our conceiving of modality (*takyif*).' The third chapter of the *Kashf* reiterates practically the same terms. It begins by saying that 'The attributes expressly used by the Sacred Book to describe the Creator and Author of the world are attributes drawn from perfections existing in man. They are seven in number: science, life, power, will, hearing, sight and language.' While discussion of the opposing arguments is left for the second part of the chapter, Ibn Rushd nevertheless states at the end of the paragraph dedicated to the first of these attributes: 'It is necessary to confess this dogma as it is given in the Revelation without saying whether God knows the origin of ephemeral beings and the corruption of corruptible beings through temporal or non-temporal science, since that constitutes an innovation within Islam.' This last charge leads us to suspect that there was a certain degree of self-interest in his attitude. Might it be the case that Ibn Rushd was seeking to clothe himself in the authority of the moment?

Moving on to the problem of divine transcendence, Ibn Rushd once again divided up what had been dealt with as a whole by Ibn Tumart – the determination of the attributes and their status. However, in this case it was primarily out of didactic concern. The Mahdi had declared at the beginning of the *Profession of faith* the order in which the questions succeeded one another:

> Religious and moral life ⟵⟶ knowledge; desire for knowledge ⟵⟶ 'promise and threat' included in the Revelation, made through the mediation of the Prophet ⟵⟶ God.

In this text he dealt only with God and in subsidiary fashion with His Messenger, and the rest of the work was left for the elaboration of *fiqh*. However, starting with the examination of the problem of divine transcendence, man did enter the picture through his attitude towards his Creator. From this point Ibn Rushd therefore emphasised the change of level: after looking into questions concerning God alone (the existence of the Creator, divine unicity, the revelation of the attributes) and having recalled that on these points the Revelation alone suffices and that nothing may be added, taken away, altered or interpreted, he turns to the Revelation as it addresses man. Only here does he take up Ibn Tumart's opposition between Creator and creature, concluding from it that the attributes common to both are possessed by the former in a manner surpassing all comprehension.

At this point it is possible to grasp what separates the two points of view. The prohibition on speculation concerning the modality of what is given by the Revelation is suddenly restricted to the common people, without Ibn Rushd feeling any need to justify this. Ibn Tumart declared of the anthropomorphic verses that 'It is necessary to believe them as they were delivered while rejecting comparison (*tashbih*) and modality (*takyif*).' Speculating on the question of the possibility of divine corporeity, Ibn Rushd concludes that on this point it is necessary to

> follow the same method as the Revelation — that is, not explicitly supporting either a negative or a positive stance, but replying to the layman who enquires upon this matter by quoting the Qur'anic verse: 'There is nothing comparable to Him. He alone sees all and hears all' (XLII.9) and by forbidding him to ask such questions.

In other words like Ibn Tumart he strove to stick to both the letter of the Text and the conclusions of rational thought. However, he did not possess the authority of the Mahdi enabling him to propound both at the same time without linking them, and he made up for this disadvantage a) positively, by borrowing from the Revelation expressions such as 'God is light' which may be understood on two levels, i.e. literally and in intellectualist fashion; b) negatively, by destroying the supposed logical implications of Kalam which only serve to sow disquiet in the spirit of men: for example, the affirmation that the existence of spatial relations in God would imply those of place. Here, the differences between the respective audiences of the two thinkers come into play. Ibn Tumart was dealing with a problem that troubled the Berber masses — that of the 'vision of God' spoken of in the Qur'an. Ibn Rushd, on the other hand, addressed a more

THE INTERPRETATION OF ALMOHADISM

cultured audience already introduced to problems of Kalam.

It is striking that Ghazali was expressly singled out here as the heir to all those who had stirred up trouble, in particular the *mutakallimun* and the Sufis. This was tantamount to designating him as the principal enemy of the Almohad position. However, since Ibn Rushd's brief summary of the work of the Eastern theologian showed that this work was designed entirely to discredit philosophy, his conclusion – though implicit – was obvious to the reader, i.e. that philosophy and Almohadism were one and the same thing. The person who departs from the text, finds ambiguities in it and tries to resolve them through allegorical interpretation, will only end up in the confusion of *ra'y* (personal opinion) already condemned by Ibn Tumart. Scholars and the uneducated masses find no ambiguity in the Revelation, but the former look at it with deliberation and immediately discover its perfect harmony with philosophy.

Finally, on the question of knowledge of divine action, Ibn Rushd groups various points of Almohad dogma in one chapter, dealing with them in his own way by relying on the idea of Providence which he used in his proof of the existence of God. First, this serves to underline the contrasting weakness of the demonstration given by Ash'arism, the *via media* of Muslim theology. It also enables him to provide a more 'comforting' justification of predestination. Ibn Tumart, obsessed with the notion of the Absolute Being, hence unchanging and hence necessary, resolved the question by saying that God is above all judgement. Ibn Rushd distinguished the powers within us which enable us to become worthy or unworthy from the external causes which influence our actions. In fact, however, there was still room for philosophical analysis of these causes to re-introduce a more or less strict determinism through the concept of Providence which was simply an interpretation of the Almohad statement that 'God produced (everything) as proof of His power and free will. He set them under Him to prove His wisdom and powers of organization.' Third, Providence helped resolve another difficulty ignored by the austere *Profession of faith* – that of the justice of creating beings for suffering. Ibn Rushd invoked the idea of 'the greatest possible good', whose Leibnizian tone softened Ibn Tumart's rigid conception of divine 'wisdom'.

However, he was forced to move closer to Ibn Tumart to resolve the difficulties in his position: including necessity in the perfection of God so as to avoid the idea that He might be subject to an external necessity; adopting the thesis that our soul is informed by the attributes and not that it projects them from man onto God, in order to criticise the idea that His actions can be neither just nor unjust.

However, on one point he does oppose the Mahdi. The latter had concluded his *Profession of faith* with the thesis of the confirmation of the prophetic mission through miracles. He was very unspecific with regard to these, but it is known that he presented himself to the masses as a miracle-worker. However, Ibn Rushd had no personal mission to justify. Far from addressing the masses, he distinguished what could be said to everyone from his philosophical work which was addressed to scholars alone. He did not evade the question of Prophecy which constitutes the second aspect of the universal Muslim profession of faith. However, in his view the only possible proof of this was the 'providential' perfection of the Qur'anic message in terms of its content rather than its form. Moreover, on no occasion does he seem to have felt the need to refer to the Mahdi as such, since the Almohad regime established an intellectual climate suitable for him – this is made evident in a famous passage praising the regime at the end of the *Fasl* – and his authority as a jurist enabled him to pronounce on what should be said to the masses while his philosophy took up the same thesis on another level of understanding.

Given the differences in approach entailed by the conception of reason as the domain of pure ideas on the one hand, and as that of cumulative knowledge on the other, Ibn Rushd thus arrived at the essential dogmas formulated by Ibn Tumart as the criteria defining his community. The difference in perspective was, as we have seen, the result of Ibn Rushd's medical training, whilst the approach of the Mahdi would have been more easily assimilated by a mathematical mind. In terms of results this only showed up in the form of certain more flexible theses, notably his insistence on Providence, which mitigated the rigid conclusions of the Berber thinker centred on necessity, and the demonstration of prophecy through the excellence of the Qur'anic doctrine alone.

The complete title of the *Kashf* is 'Exposition of the methods of demonstration relative to the dogmas of religion, and definition of the equivocations and innovations which appear in them as methods of interpretation and which distort the truth or lead into error' (trans. R. Arnaldez, *Encyclopédie de l'Islam*). Thus the work was envisaged primarily as a polemic, and its refutations provide

THE INTERPRETATION OF ALMOHADISM

many items of information on the history of religious ideas – with the constant exception of the mu'tazilite school whose works he claimed not to have come across in Spain.

The *Fasl al-maqal* is the best-known work, and chronologically it predates the *Kashf*. The preamble of the *Kashf* mentions the *Fasl*, saying that since that work demonstrated that the Revelation includes one part that is clear and one requiring interpretation, the present work will be dedicated to examining the former, which applies to all men. Once an examination of the *Kashf* has revealed the motives of the author we can turn to this methodological introduction to philosophico-religious thought.

It is the Qur'an itself that invites rational study of things (cf. LIX–2, VII–184). 'Truth cannot contradict truth' and it is therefore legitimate to 'unite what is given by reason (*ma'qul*) and that which is provided by tradition (*manqul*)'. To accomplish this, Ibn Rushd adopted the distinction drawn by the mystics between apparent meaning (*zahir*) and hidden meaning (*batin*), with allegorical interpretation (*ta'wil*) as a corollary. However, this form of interpretation remained within the framework of Almohad rationalism and aimed simply to avoid the impieties and heresies arising from anthropomorphism. (1) It is only possible if the words of the text taken in their literal sense do not have an obvious meaning. Some dogmas whose expression presents no linguistic problems are thus outside its field and fall within the province of literal commentary (*tafsir* – a word used frequently to describe Ibn Rushd's large commentaries on Aristotle). Moreover, it was on these that the *Kashf* focuses. (2) It has to adhere strictly to the normal rules of the Arabic language concerning metaphors. (3) Its application depends both on the intellectual level of those persons involved and the type of metaphor in question. If the idea expressed by the image is difficult to grasp, interpretation is only permitted to the most scholarly individuals. If it is very easy to grasp, everyone is required to study it. If it is clear that an image is involved but that it remains obscure, then this is because God's aim is to move the heart rather than transmit knowledge – only scholars can look for its true meaning, and for others it is better either to refrain altogether or to content themselves with the easiest interpretation. Finally, if it is easy to find the sense of the metaphor eventually but not evident that a metaphor is involved, then it is necessary either to abstain or to adopt the allegorical interpretation corresponding to one's degree of doubt. These last two points were directed against the excesses of the Sufis and rash allegories which did not do justice to the Revelation. On this point Ibn Rushd was only too happy to be able to appeal to the rules of caution laid down by Ghazali and even considered it necessary to be more discriminating than him.

The *Fasl* applied an argumentation which had been prepared in the juridical methodology of the *Bidaya*. In the *Bidaya* Ibn Rushd preferred to use the expression *al-kalam al-fiqhi* (juridical discourse) to indicate its close link with apologetic theology (i.e. Kalam) and he insisted on the role of reasoning in both. On the problem of juridical consensus (*ijma'*), he refused to search for this in the practice of the Companions of the Prophet, and even in the utterances of one of the Companions not invalidated by the others. In his opinion, consensus was reached 'once the question has been widely aired and no differences of opinion concerning it are known to us' (R. Brunschvig, p.48). Thus, there was an appeal to universal reason rather than incidental historical considerations.

It is reason itself which obliges us to resort to reasoning by analogy (*qiyas*) in matters of practice, since the texts, like the Prophet's actions and silences of approbation, are limited in number, whilst the number of possible cases is unlimited. As in the thought of Ibn Tumart, it is reason that opposes the positive character of the Law to the speculative nature of belief. The *Fasl al-maqal* takes up this idea that *qiyas* draws on opinion (*zann*) which must yield in the presence of a revealed text and which also lacks the apodictic properties of philosophical syllogism (also termed *qiyas*). However, Ibn Rushd did not therefore deny the need for it in the sphere of everyday practice.

To summarize, the classical Islamic distinction between the masses (*'amma*) and the educated elite (*khassa*) explains the difference in perspective between the *shari'a* (religious Law) which is addressed to all, and philosophy which is the exclusive domain of the educated. There is no contradiction between the two so long as false problems (Kalam) or false solutions (sufism) are not invented. R. Brunschvig has commented that the *Bidaya* concludes by constructing 'a bridge between *fiqh* and morality' (p.65): legal precepts aspire to promote the virtues of temperance, justice, courage and generosity. The *Fasl* goes even further in this, but adopts a polemical tone, deploring the fact that the jurists have corrupted their discipline by turning it into an instrument of profit or power.

THE INTERPRETATION OF ALMOHADISM

It is in this context that the problem of reconciling faith and reason should be tackled. Renan distorted the problem by presenting it in Western terms, forgetting that for a Muslim faith is above all a form of *practice*. Just as the Mahdi created a gradated order of adherence to his doctrine ranging from the simplest 'guides' to the complex 'Profession', so Ibn Rushd stated that ordinary religion is sufficient for the masses while philosophy is needed to satisfy the educated individual. There is no opposition between the two, but neither is any communication possible between the symbolic language intended for the former and the demonstrative language of the latter. Here we come across the traditional Islamic element of the study of the arcane and at the same time the Aristotelian classification of arguments according to the level of the minds involved. In the light of this we can appreciate Ibn Rushd's sincerity when he acknowledged that his most painful experience occurred one day when he entered the mosque with his son and was thrown out by a turbulent horde. Here we see not only the humiliation of an eminent figure, but also his deep sense of outrage at the intrusion of the uneducated into a sphere which did not belong to them.

There was also the problem of the apologetic theologians. The Aristotelian classification mentioned above was a tripartite one, and in the *Fasl* Ibn Rushd permits consideration of the dialectic outlook. However, by replacing this work in perspective as we have, it becomes clear that Ibn Rushd was not content to insert this category in an intermediate position between the two others. On this point alone we can perhaps accept Renan's comment that his aim was to allay suspicions. The basic feeling of the philosopher was that the semi-rationalist, semi-fideist outlook of the theologians only helped distort the facts. The *Fasl* is not as explicit on this subject as the *Kashf*, but it clearly emphasises, for example, the disagreements of the *mutakallimun* concerning the life to come.

However, Ibn Rushd ran up against questions not faced by the Mahdi when he formulated his gradated system. Ghazali had cast explicit doubts on *Falsafa* as originally formulated, in particular on the theses of the eternity of the world, and of the non-existence of God's eternal knowledge of particular things, etc.. Ibn Rushd proceeded in two stages. First, he got round the problem of the unbelief of the ancient *Falasifa* using a juridical argument: the *takfir* (charge of unbelief) directed against them cannot have been intended 'in an absolute sense' but only 'as a measure of severity'.

79

Then he shows that Ghazali misunderstood the questions of doctrine. Here he anticipates the *Tahafut al-tahafut* which was itself explicitly conceived as a response to Ghazali's *Tahafut al-falasifa* (Incoherence of the philosophers, against which was directed the Incoherence of the incoherence).

The significance of the *Tahafut* is two-fold. On the one hand, it follows through the conclusions of the critique of Ghazali outlined in the two previous texts, and even extends to a methodical refutation of long passages quoted from the text. If this critique is the most obvious element common to all three texts, this is doubtless due to the large number of people in al-Andalus at the time who, as we have seen, were attracted by the syncretism which had already manifested itself on several occasions and which, paradoxically, succeeded in imposing itself from within Almohadism itself. On the other hand, Ibn Rushd used Almohadism to resolve the problem of the position taken by Ibn Tufayl who had claimed to reconcile Ibn Sina and Ghazali through esoterism. Far from providing justification for al-Farabi and Ibn Sina in the face of Ghazali's criticisms, Ibn Rushd's aim in refuting these criticisms was to eliminate those who might have inspired them and to return beyond the errors of Eastern *Falsafa* to true philosophy.

The *Tahafut* corrects any elements of abruptness there may have been in the *Fasl*, and in particular affirms the superiority of a religion based on *both* reason and Revelation over a religion based on reason alone. Yet this was only an extension of the theory of Prophethood found in the *Fasl*, where the Prophet was seen as one who had received from the active Intellect not only rational forms of thought like the philosophers, but also the power to translate them through the use of imagination into symbols with a hold over the common people.

He also adopted a pragmatic attitude already found in other *Falasifa* who considered it a good idea to borrow precepts from religions. This prompted his insistence on the Qur'anic doctrine and presentation of Islam as the last and best in a series of revelations – a doctrine not explicitly mentioned in the *Fasl*.

Hence, the polemic on the subject of Ibn Rushd's 'rationalism' seems weak in its presentation, despite the subtleties contributed by L. Gauthier and then M. Alonso. The *Tahafut* defines the limits of human reason, admits that the principles of religion *as a historical phenomenon* surpass the intelligence of man, recognises the existence of miracles, etc.. Indeed, it follows the same procedure as

Ibn Tumart's *Profession of faith*, which, having established a chain of reasons leading to God as the Absolute Being, states, 'Here lies the extreme limit of knowledge'. Similarly, it concludes with an affirmation of the truthfulness of the Prophet on the strength of the miracles he performed. There is no doubt that Ibn Rushd belonged to that *madhab al-fikr* 'doctrine of the Logos' of Almohadism denounced by the traditionalists. He is not a rationalist in the reductive sense of a thinker like Renan, but rather in the sense that applied to his contemporaries, even non-Muslims such as Saint Anselm. Certainly, there is a degree of this in the latter, Ibn Rushd's thought being 'less a *fides quaerens intellectum* than a perfect faith which embraces a rational knowledge' (Arnaldez, *Encyclopédie de l'Islam*).

Almohadism affirmed that man is capable of reconstructing the chain of reasons, but that this work is undertaken *a posteriori*. This is why Ibn Tumart confirmed his deductions with quotations from the Revelation. It was this too that prompted Ibn Tufayl's wish to follow up the shipwreck adventure of Hayy, by confronting this experience, which could not have been more 'exceptional', with the common norm represented by the character of Asal. Ibn Rushd's *Fasl* affirms the possibility and legitimacy of an approach based on reason, but does not affirm that this is the only acceptable path and even less that it is possible without the existence of other ones. However, it is true that the *Tahafut* is alone in stating this final point, saying that

> just as the elite class of people (i.e. the philosophers) does not exist and cannot attain happiness without the participation of the general populace, so general education is necessary to the existence of the elite class and to its life: certainly with regards to the period of its childhood and its upbringing; and with regards to the time of its passage towards that which makes it elite, it is necessary for the sake of excellence not to spurn that in which it rises, and that it proceed to that point by resorting to the best of interpretations.
>
> (ed. Bouyges, p.582)

THE PHILOSOPHICAL IMPLICATIONS

To interpret Almohadism in philosophical terms was not an automatic step, despite the fundamentally philosophical nature of Ibn Tumart's thought. We have already seen Ibn Tufayl's failure in this respect – a result of his desire to reconcile the structure of the Mahdi's thought with the *pre-existing* philosophico-cultural milieu. This explains the character of his project which was both fascinating and absurd, and in which the worst confusions of syncretism co-existed with brilliant intuitions (for example, on the unity and continuity of the species) which, however, were not investigated in any depth.

This seems to explain Ibn Rushd's fervent adherence to Aristotle. It was he who had the courage to break with a tradition that had been influential far more as a result of its continuity than for the minor corrections brought by individual thinkers. Moreover, he belonged to a civilization in which the concept of the individual problematic did not exist (in the whole of *Falsafa* Abu Bakr al-Razi was perhaps the only person capable of thinking outside the framework of the authorities, and the conditions in which his personal thought was elaborated were completely different from those of Ibn Rushd, though he did borrow a great deal from Antiquity). The only solution that remained open to him was to go even further than the principal authority recognised by all the *Falasifa* (except Razi, that is) while retaining his freedom by stating the need to restore this authority in its purest form. In this way, he directly called into question the old accusation of *tahrif* (altering a Revelation, which had been levelled against the Jews and Christians, whose authenticity is now restored), and also the reaction of all Islamic reform movements to deviations and innovations (*bid'a*).

The *Tahafut al-tahafut* constituted a synthesis of Ibn Rushd's religious concerns and the contributions of the first series of commentaries. The work attempted to strike a balance between peripatetic philosophy and the Qur'anic Revelation interpreted by the Mahdi, sacrificing nothing of one to the other while satisfactorily embracing of *both*.

It starts out with the question of creation. The *shahada* – the Muslim profession of faith – simply proclaims the unicity of God, and the Qur'an is not explicit concerning the process of creation. R. Arnaldez has underlined the fact that 'the idea of creation *ex nihilo* is not expressed in the Qur'an; it has to be inserted in order to find it there' ('La Pensée religieuse d'Averroes' I, p.101). Rather, the text gives the impression of an organization and the verbs used can be interpreted either in absolute or relative sense. In the *Fasl*, Ibn Rushd did not hesitate to employ such a distinction.

THE INTERPRETATION OF ALMOHADISM

However, Muslim theological tradition has always insisted on another aspect of the Revelation – the idea of the total submission of the universe to God. Ghazali, following Ash'arite Kalam, deduced from this a theory of the attributes which established a personal relationship between God and the world. However, he was not content to draw a simplistic opposition between 'time' and 'before time', since he agreed with the *Falasifa* in believing that the nature of eternity is not infinite time but a mode of being particular to the transcendent Being.

The traditional argument positing the existence of the Creator starting from the observation of the existence of the contingent, hence of the created, had also been modified by Ibn Tumart. The latter did not see a personal link between the two terms so much as a logical relation:

> the act cannot exist without the one who performs it, there is no doubt concerning the existence of the latter (. . .) and the existence of that from which doubt is removed is necessarily known. It is thus proved that the Creator is known by the necessity of reason.
>
> *(Profession of faith*, para. 1)

Ghazali and Ibn Tumart were thus united in the opinion that the problem of the creation is fundamental, but the former directs it towards a critique of the thesis of the eternity of the world, whilst the latter implicitly dismisses this question by transforming it on the level of logic. The creation does not oppose two temporalities but two qualifications.

> Man knows necessarily that the water from which he has been created possessed a single quality incorporating neither difference, nor composition, nor form, nor bone, nor flesh, nor auditory faculty, nor visual faculty and in which all these qualities were subsequently found after they had not existed.
>
> *(Profession of faith*, para. 2)

This 'primordial water' is thus pure potential. Creation consists in giving it a form. Transposed onto the level of the 'measurement' of time by the movement of the spheres, this provides the solution proposed by Ibn Rushd to the objections of Ghazali. Against al-Farabi's idea that the world is not eternal because it is temporal by nature, temporality being the mode of being of beings, the theologian states that in a vision of the world made up of concentric spheres one merely shifts the problem, the movement of one sphere supposing the movement of another, and the whole process extending back to infinity. Ibn Rushd simply points out that if time is measured in terms of movement inasmuch as the latter can be calculated because it has a beginning and an end, when it relates to revolutions past or to come it is simply in the soul and is pure potential to be calculated. And, 'What is potential is equal to nothingness' (*Tahafut*, ed. Bouyges, p.24).

Ibn Tumart's argument gets round the problem of time because his aim is completely different. His proof of the existence of the Creator implies that the created thing cannot be a creator itself and thus God is completely beyond comparison; the Mahdi's main objective is to establish this 'absolute' nature. Ibn Rushd, however, had to reply to specific objections and could not proceed so rapidly. This prompted him initially to bring the question of time onto the level of the action of a being in actuality on a potential being, in other words, onto the level of particulars or of the action of the upper spheres on them. However, in challenging the emanatist schema and the continuity it implies, he remained wholly within the Almohad perspective in which the act of creation lay in the absolute transcendence of God over what He produces, which has no resemblance to Him.

If, as Ghazali would have it, God innovated in His eternal will in establishing the world in the time in which it exists, this would imply that God is subject to temporality since He would have to create in time, and so changes His will. According to Ibn Tumart, '(. . .) those who have knowledge of divine acts (. . .) have ruled out modality (*takyif*) from divine majesty, since it would lead to anthropomorphism and to atheism' (para. 8). That is why, Ibn Rushd continues, one cannot truly speak of the will of God except to avoid a false idea; similarly, his science is not what we call a universal science; etc. At times, therefore, the *Tahafut* takes up and enlarges upon the analyses of the *Kashf*, still with the same explicit objective of not upsetting the 'sense of the divine' (*ma'na al-ilahiya*) (p.356) possessed by the common people.

It is permitted to speak by means of an image as long as this is not an empty rhetorical formula but an indirect path to knowledge. This applies to the idea of will which serves to demonstrate the transcendence of God with regard to His creation. Similarly, the relation between the movement of the celestial bodies and their principle is expressed by Ibn Rushd as a command (*amr*). This term is not wholly satisfactory but is the only one able to explain the action of that which is separate from matter on matter. Moreover, this image is informative regarding the nature of the celestial bodies since it implies that they 'are rational beings that have consciousness of their own essence and also their motivating principles in the manner of an order given to them' (*Tah.*, pp.184–5).

The application of the Aristotelian schema also led him to distinguish two things: on the one hand is the world as an effect of divine action, thus linked to him and without beginning or end. This can be explained – bearing in mind its subordinate nature in relation to the eternal – by saying that it is 'with time'. On the other hand are the creatures of the world that are 'in time'.

God creates the metaphysical compound of matter and form and agents intervene to make that which was in a state of potential pass into actuality or to annihilate it. Nothingness is thus second in relation to existence. Hence, strictly speaking, there cannot be creation *ex nihilo*. This implicitly harks back to Ibn Tumart's formula cited above, describing the appearance of qualities in pure potential which, moreover, is not matter since that only exists in the compound of matter and form.

The anteriority of existence thus leads to a rebuttal of Ibn Sina's distinction between the necessary being and the possible being. Ghazali limited himself to saying that this was not clear since the two beings are not on the same level. Ibn Rushd particularly emphasises that this distinction is purely notional. If the subordination of the possible to the necessary is internal to the latter, the possible becomes necessary as soon as the necessary being exists. This is acknowledged by Ibn Sina, but it was not acceptable to Ibn Tumart who uses necessity only on the level of logical inference ('this necessity is autonomous in the souls of all beings endowed with reason' (para. 2)) and who consequently finds necessity in the characteristics of existence itself (as the following argument demonstrates: '. . . of whomsoever the beginning, the end, the delimitation and the particularization are necessary, the place he occupies in space, the alteration, the contingency, the particularization, the adventitiousness and the need for a Creator are necessary' (para. 7)).

On the one hand, Ibn Rushd criticises the definition of the necessary as that which has no cause and of the possible as that which does have one, and brings the question onto another level.

Only for compound beings is there equivalence between the nature of being possible and that of being caused, for no compound is eternal. But if all beings without cause are necessary, that does not signify that all necessary beings are without cause. There are beings that are at once necessary, because they are eternal, and dependent on the primary cause.

On the other hand, for Ibn Rushd, these characteristics of existence naturally correspond to the ten categories of Aristotelian logic, of which the being is 'like the genus'.

> The essential meaning (of the word 'existence') which refers to things which exist in the real world outside the soul is prior to the sense it has in the existents from the second intention, and it is this sense which is predicated of the ten categories analogically, and it is in this sense that we say of the substance that it exists by itself, and of the accident that it exists through its existing in the existent which subsists by itself.
>
> (*Tah.*, p.303)

In not starting from the concrete being, Ibn Sina established his negation of the independent reality of the divine attributes on a poor basis. For Ibn Rushd the best method was still that of the Mu'tazilites (taken up by Ibn Tumart) who move back from the possible reality towards a First Principle 'which is the final term in the series of possibilities and is not a possibility, which implies its absolute simplicity' (*Tah.*, p. 321). God is the necessary Being *with regard to* the beings of the world, but we cannot pronounce on what He is in Himself. As Ibn Tumart put it: 'Conjecture does not extend to Him, nor does reason give Him form' (para. 7).

On the other hand, thought does intervene to distinguish attributes in God in relation to actions *ad extra*. These attributes are based on the perfection of essence, but are to a greater extent attributes of action. Thus multiplicity is internal, but in a manner different to our own, which is due to the action of the numerical multiplicity of concrete objects. In particular, divine science does not proceed through abstraction, which is the act of man. If God has a knowledge of particulars, it is not through a particular science, but in His capacity as a Creator who possesses absolutely within Himself everything He has created, and what exists is the diversity of the particular. The same is true of the other attributes: willpower, power, etc. extend to the particulars in a manner

THE INTERPRETATION OF ALMOHADISM

inaccessible to human understanding. All this is nothing other than a development of the Mahdi's formula: 'the Creator is necessarily living, knowing, powerful, endowed with willpower, hearing, sight, speech, and all this without our conceiving of modality' (para. 10). Thus it in fact constituted a union between the philosophical discussion of the critiques of Ghazali and the Eastern *Falasifa* on the one hand, and religious belief on the other. As such, R. Arnaldez was correct in stating that 'the thought of Averroes is religious, like that of Saint Thomas, of Spinoza, and Leibniz, whatever differences may emerge' ('La Pensée religieuse d'Averroes' II, p.28).

While Almohad ideology permitted an 'understanding' of the Revelation in philosophical terms, these terms were not neutral and were to lead Ibn Rushd far beyond the framework of the Profession of faith. Thus the Mahdi spoke in terms of cause, and Ibn Rushd always returned to the presentation of God as cause. But Aristotle taught that this term is ambiguous and describes the agent, the form, the matter and the end (*Tah.*, p.226). Ibn Rushd's reasoning thus ultimately posited God, not just as 'he who makes all things come from nothingness into existence and who preserves them' (*Tah.*, p.151), but also as 'the cause of the realization of potential beings in beings in actuality' (p.240), and cause of the order (*tartib*) of the world inasmuch as he is its finality, and in particular of the movement of the spheres (pp.176 and 185).

If God is the cause of sensible forms it is in His role as intelligence. At this point Ibn Rushd can no longer simply 'encompass' Aristotle in the context of Almohad Islam, but has to correct him. Aristotle presented God as incapable of thinking beings inferior to Himself, but only of thinking Himself (*noesis noeseos*), and Ghazali deduced from this that He was unaware of what He had created. To this Ibn Rushd replied that 'this only follows if what he thinks of himself is something other than beings in their absolute existence' (*Tah.*, p.226). This thought is the creator of its own objects which are none other than 'existing things in their most noble existence' (*Tah.*, p.226); Ibn Rushd explains this term giving the example of colour which exists initially in matter, then in the sight, then in the imagination, in memory and finally in the intelligence.

The question of the life to come does not appear in the Almohad Profession of faith, nor in the first *murshida* but only in the second, and then in an appendix which does not appear in all versions. The passage which deals literally with the themes of judgement, the interrogation of the soul by two angels, the bridge, the scales, etc., has clear Hanbali tones which contrast with that of the texts as a whole. It is impossible to say whether it is interpolated or not, but it is indicative of a need to complete – at least for the common people – the speculation on the only two explicit aspects of the *shahada*: the unicity of God and the prophetic mission. Ghazali stated that the philosophical solution, which reserves immortality for separate spirits, contradicts belief in the resurrection and in tangible rewards. Ibn Rushd's approach under these circumstances only aimed initially to demonstrate the falsity of the doubts voiced by Ghazali against the arguments of the *Falasifa*. However, later, feeling the need for coherence, he tried with this redoubled criticism to construct a theory that could be reconciled with Aristotelianism.

First, he turns to Aristotle's idea that only the intellect is spiritual and therefore immortal, but with an impersonal immortality, since it is alien to all that is individual. Concerning the other aspects of the soul, linked to an organ of perception, one can at the most conjecture that the organ can grow weak without power being affected. Only scholars unshakeable (*rasikhun*) in their science have received from God the ability to see into this question, because they know the limits of thought. The Revelation itself presents an image (Qur'an, XXXIX, 43): That of sleep. In sleep the soul has no activity because it does not make use of the organs, and yet it subsists. This is more than an image, it is a sign (*dalil*). On the question of immortality, Ibn Rushd makes a change in method: he no longer follows Ghazali step by step, but summarizes him, and does not refer in person to Aristotle who could be of no help to him. Instead he gives an account of the various philosophical solutions put forward since Antiquity. He suggests justifications for these opinions indicating that he considers them to be images ultimately reconcilable with the images of the Revelation.

Resurrection is a question that does not come into philosophy, but one in which all the Islamic philosophers believed. It encourages virtue. This is not just true for the common people, but also for wise men who need the moral virtues in order to realize the contemplative virtues. Ibn Rushd quotes two traditions that he interprets to mean 'that our existence there is another

THE INTERPRETATION OF ALMOHADISM

creation, superior to this existence' (*Tah.*, p.585), our new bodies being 'likenesses (*amthal*) of our own'.

3

A 'HUMAN' KNOWLEDGE

We have distinguished in the work of Ibn Rushd a period of scientific preparation and a period during which he formulated his religious thought. There was no clean break between this and the work that followed, since coinciding with this second period and extending beyond it up until the end of Ibn Rushd's life, was a third phase dedicated to the highly detailed study of the field of knowledge. Structurally, this field was as he had inherited it from the editors of Aristotle, but at the same time it was subject to the two opposing and complementary corrections already distinguished – i.e. suppression of neoplatonic and other additions, but acceptance of complementary work and developments which Ibn Rushd considered in keeping with the spirit of the work.

The stages dating from this period are:

In 572/1177 Ibn Rushd concluded the cycle of commentaries devoted to Aristotle with his middle commentary on the *Nichomachean Ethics*. At the same time he announced that since Aristotle's *Politics* were unknown in Spain but, he believed, known in the East, he would turn his attention if possible to this work. At this point his contribution to practical philosophy ended for a period – and indeed was not picked up until seventeen years later.

In 573/1178: *Sermo de Substantia Orbis*

In 582/1186: *Tafsir* (large commentary) on the *Physics*

In 589/1193: *Talkhis* on Galen's *Treatise on Fevers*

In 590/1194: *Talkhis* on Plato's *Republic*

In 591/1195 (during his period of disgrace): Questions of logic (on the *Prior Analytics*).

These dates are limited in number, but are nevertheless sufficient to bring out two important facts: the brief and middle commentaries were continued but, since Aristotle's own work had

90

A 'HUMAN' KNOWLEDGE

already been covered, these only dealt with complementary works likely to be accepted (such as Plato's politics and Galen). Sarton has also suggested that a middle commentary on *De Anima* be dated 577/1181. However, he is the only one to hold this view. M. Alonso follows the traditional order, inclining more towards 569/1173 and in any case before the commentary on the *Metaphysics* (c.570/1174) and those on morality.

Those works not falling into the categories of the three types of commentary are inserted to enlarge upon points Ibn Rushd clearly found particularly interesting. With regard to these works which were called *masa'il* and dealt with logic, it is possible to suggest that Ibn Rushd was embarking on a fourth stage of his work. However, this is still a matter for conjecture.

In terms of quantity, though, this period is most significant for the large commentaries (*tafsir* or *sharh*) in which Ibn Rushd's instruction goes into minute detail. The scope of these works is difficult to define. While Latin scholars of Averroes considered them the pure thought of the master, it has been pointed out that Ibn Rushd was often content simply to collect the opinions of other commentators. Even more important is a major piece of evidence that can be taken from the author's own middle commentary on the *Physics*:

> What we have written on these matters, we have only done so in order to provide an interpretation of the meaning of the Peripatetics so as to facilitate their understanding for those who wish to know these things. We have taken as our aim the same as that of Abu Hamid (Ghazali) in his book on the *Maqasid* (*Intentions of the Philosophers* – a neutral presentation preparing the critique of the *Tahafut*); for if one does not examine in depth the opinions of men at their very source, one cannot recognise the errors attributed to them, nor distinguish them from the truth.
>
> (*Aristotelis opera omnia cum Averrois Commentariis*, vol. IV, f.146 v.)

Experts have been able to pick out scattered expressions which indicate that the author is giving his own opinion, but these are generally on points of detail which are difficult to place in coherent order. Therefore, in the absence of a system, we shall try to determine the essential corner-stones of Rushdian philosophy.

REASONING

Ibn Rushd's own scientific works reiterate the need to possess not only empirical knowledge, but also the art of Logic. His religious work insistently opposes the conjectural reasoning of the Mutakallimun to genuine proof (*burhan*). His final work was a reconsideration of particular problems of logic, and represented a true statement of principle at a time when he was derided with the title of *Mutafalsif*. Yet analysts from Gauthier to Gilson have refused to believe that there is a genuine Rushdian contribution to Logic. In response to this, publication and translation efforts have been undertaken over the past few years which, despite some lack of order and numerous repetitions (see bibliography) have finally drawn attention to the brief and middle commentaries on the *Organon*. Unfortunately, of the large commentaries only that on the *Posterior Analytics* is known and at present almostly solely in dubious Hebrew and Latin translations that are often largely incomprehensible.

Ibn Rushd's outlook is characterized firstly by its strictness. Although he agreed to make a commentary on the *Isagoge* of Porphyry, this was to meet the request of friends. He did not consider the work an introduction to Logic as it had been universally accepted up until that time, except by al-Farabi in his *Classification of the Sciences* (*Ihsa al-'Ulum*). However, the reasons of the two may have differed, since Farabi considered Logic as that which governs the sciences by pronouncing on the true and the false, whereas Ibn Rushd maintained its autonomy with respect to the theoretical and practical sciences and made it into a basic discipline at the service of the others.

In his work Porphyry gives the definitions of the five fundamental concepts of genus, species, specific difference, property, and accident, and in the course of the five chapters considers the particular concepts in terms of their resemblance or difference. However, unlike Aristotle for whom species is not a predicable but the subject which receives the predicables, Porphyry makes species into an attribute and considers it equivalent to the definition. Moreover, the status of these concepts is not fixed in his thought: since in certain attributions the genus and the species can substitute for one another he maintains that the two notions are relative. Furthermore, he questions whether genera and species exist in reality or only in the spirit, though he fails to provide an answer.

These aspects, which distance Porphyry's approach from Aristotelian logic and which explain why he was rejected by Ibn Rushd, demonstrate his rejection of dispersion in favour of clearly delimited subjects. Similarly, in the elaboration of knowledge, he distinguishes what he considers genuinely scientific arguments from dialectical ones. The latter are needed in order to embark upon research, set forth questions and proceed by trial and error in the pursuit of demonstration. However, once this goal is achieved everything preceding it can be discarded. This remark, made with regard to the study of the Sky and the world (*Al-Sama wa-al-'alam*, pp.2–3) leads, in the middle commentary on the *Topics*, to the idea that dialectic does not have its own independent sphere, as Aristotle believed, but is only useful for demonstration and for political use. Induction does not serve, as Aristotle states, to reveal the first principles of an art, but simply to verify the universal principles of dialectic syllogisms. It is thus comparable to rhetorical examples or poetic images, and dialectic can barely be differentiated from debate. Only syllogisms and definitions can give first principles.

However, things are not as simple as these declarations of principle might suggest. While adopting Aristotle's analysis of probative discourse in literal fashion, Ibn Rushd emphasises various points which give a particular tone to his logical theory. His starting point is the question of the ontological foundations of knowledge. Thought starts from principles which it cannot employ as it pleases, as in sophistry. The latter is not just the work of certain perverse individuals, it also has cultural aspects. In his commentary on the *Sophistical Refutations* (*Safsata*) Ibn Rushd was prompted on several occasions to pick out literary formulae fully codified and commented upon in the Arab tradition, such as metaphor, metonymy, analogy, synecdoche, etc., in order to demonstrate the moral dangers they contained.

We have seen (Ch.1, para. 3) how Ibn Rushd integrated Rhetoric as a phenomenon of communication, and in due course we will see the place he gives it amongst the lower forms of political pedagogy. There is a tension here between the philosopher's desire to take into account the whole of reality, starting with his own cultural milieu, and that of the technician whose task it is to expose error and even risks of error. This second position can be maintained in two different ways. The first is that chosen by Ibn Bajja who sticks exclusively to Aristotelian logic and at the same time isolates his 'solitary' from the cultural framework. However, there is another approach represented by an almost exact contemporary of Ibn Rushd, Ibn Mada' (513/1119–592/1195) who was born in Cordoba, died in Seville, and was Qadi of North Africa and then supreme Qadi of the whole Almohad Empire. The respective offices of Ibn Mada and Ibn Rushd must have brought them into contact with one another. He stands quite alone in this period, and his *Refutation of the Grammarians* is far ahead of its time. Its modern character is proved by the fact that it was later published only by Shawqi Dayf,[1] which suggests that it could serve as a basis for a new formulation of Arabic grammar.

Everything seems to suggest that Ibn Mada had taken note of the integration of the problems of comprehension into philosophy, restricting himself to language in the strict sense of the word. While Ibn Rushd pushes Almohadism towards scientific rationalism, Ibn Mada' picks up on the religious orientation of the movement, and moves towards another kind of rationalism – that of Ibn Hazm. The only works attributed to him by the biographers are three books of grammar, and only the one mentioned above has reached us. Besides the author's obvious reliance on Ibn Tumart's methodological rules, it is possible to pick out other aspects of Almohad ideology implicit in his work – his profound spirituality, his taste for broad outlines which might be likened to the 'large-scale decor' found in the plastic arts of the period, his hostility to the hypocrisy of the jurists and the casuistry of the soul, and finally his independence from the oriental heritage. Above all, there are parallels between the paths followed by Ibn Rushd and Ibn Mada' in the name of Almohadism: on the one hand is the philosopher who adopts the perspective of the rational theology of the Mahdi, and rejects apologetic theology as arbitrary and uncertain in favour of philosophy of which he considers Aristotelianism the most apodictic form. On the other, we find the grammarian, who follows the same methodology, applying it to the language of the Revelation, and rejects the extra-grammatical considerations of his colleagues in favour of an analysis of the materiality of the text, the theory and example of which had been provided by Ibn Hazm.

Ibn Mada's criticism of the artificial constructions of the grammarians is radical. In order to justify the phenomenon of rection, or grammatical action of one word on another, they assume the existence of something beyond words themselves. To account for the cases of words in a complex phrase, they assume the existence of implied terms which would govern the apparently anomalous cases – which is a way of complicating the language with an artificial construction rather than analysing it in itself. Lastly, to explain the causes of grammatical phenomena they use the juridical type of analogy, whereas Ibn Mada' follows the line of Zahirism – the literalist school of Ibn Hazm – and challenges this analogy, seeing no other cause for the facts than their existence itself and the usage in which they are involved. Appeal to the consciousness of the speaker and the interlocutor alike is thus fundamentally excluded for fear of rendering the language defective – which is inadmissible for an Arab – and the meaning is entirely in the materiality of the word.

Here, the difference between Zahirism and Almohadism is even greater than in the field of *fiqh*. While both oppose the arbitrary intervention of the 'opinion' of the ulema in determining the rules of life, Almohadism adheres to the necessities of practice whereas Zahirism goes as far as possible in excluding everything that is not in the body of the discourse itself. The immediate consequence of this is that Zahirism remained a scholarly exercise practised by a small elite of a particularly scrupulous and rigorous outlook on the level of logic, whereas Almohadism was able to integrate logic but at the same time keep a hold on the people by inciting them to action by means of stirring myths.

Thus Ibn Rushd views language as both misleading and inescapable. It has to be taken into account, but not taken as the ultimate source of reference. The only possible solution is to look into the field of the application of language. Here we find a second ontological principle, namely that principles develop into arguments which are a conjunction of matter and form. Thought is a form which requires the existence of a material substratum. One thing and its opposite cannot exist in a being at the same time – hence the principle: We cannot think two possible opposites at the same time.

It is thus *temporality* that constitutes the reference point of the probative argument. In one of the *Questions of Logic* – his final works – Ibn Rushd declares: 'The aim of this discourse is to investigate the (type of) premise called *assertoric* or *absolute* – what it is and what is the teaching of Aristotle about this (matter). For the commentators differ about this. . . .' (trans. N. Rescher: 'Averroes' *Quaesitum* on assertoric propositions', p.94). In particular he contrasts the ancient Peripatetics (Theophrastus, Eudemus and

Themistius) to Alexander of Aphrodisias and his followers, in particular al-Farabi. The thesis of the former boils down to the idea that an assertoric premise has no modality of possibility or necessity, whereas matter must necessarily have one or the other. The assertoric mode thus appears as a sort of class of which the necessary and the possible could be either one or the other kind — the kind being determined by the subject. For Alexander of Aphrodisias, on the other hand, the assertoric proposition would be possible if its content existed in fact. In other words, Ibn Rushd adds, 'when it is actually found that the predicate belongs to the subject, that is, at the present time' (p.95). The first group objected to this saying that the proposition is no longer universal, 'but only asserts by chance and for the least time' (p.96). Aristotle gave a directive, in the study of the modally mixed syllogism, 'to avoid these kinds of absolutes, and to employ the absolute which is not limited temporally' (p.96). Alexander in turn replied that his opponents' theory introduced an absolute that existed only in the intellect and not in fact. On the other hand, in an opposing syllogism Aristotle himself often changed a possible premise into an assertoric premise.

Ibn Rushd's solution is to systematize the considerations of temporality which were introduced by his predecessors with purely polemic objectives (Rescher thinks it possible that there was a stoic influence on these ancient polemics). A proposition is universal if its predicate belongs to all the subjects; but this can be so in two ways: (A) actually (B) not actually but simply as a possibility, 'I mean in *future time*' (p.98). The first can in turn be divided into:

(A) – The predicate is *always* present in the subject (= necessary)
   – The predicate is sometimes but not always present in the subject (which is the assertoric proposition and in turn divides:)
   – The predicate is present *most of the time* in the subject.
   – The predicate is present *half the time* in the subject.
   – The predicate is present *for a lesser part of the time* in the subject.

These last three formulae are identical to the possible (B).

Ibn Rushd starts by stating that possibility is linked to the viewpoint of the subject, and not of the time, but that the assertoric character itself is linked solely to the viewpoint of time. Nevertheless, straight after that he gives a temporal quantification

A 'HUMAN' KNOWLEDGE

of possibility itself, and eliminates from the scientific language the final category (actual predicate for the lesser part of the time, and possible most of the time).

In this way Ibn Rushd proposes a solution which accounts for the two different references made to Aristotle, and at the same time unilaterally explains the two facts invoked by means of a third point of view. However, he immediately acknowledges that this is his own point of view and not explicitly Aristotle's: 'I mean that he did not differentiate in this book (*The Prior Analytics*) the mostlys from the leastlys. We have already dicussed the reasons for this in our Middle Commentary on this book (Book I, Ch.13)' (p.102).

The significance of this use of temporality goes considerably beyond the one specific problem invoked in this opuscule. At the end of the work, Ibn Rushd devotes a kind of appendix to refuting Ibn Sina's position, which corresponds to neither of those envisaged above and which he describes as 'very obscure'. Ibn Sina brings in both temporality and necessity (as he understands it). Not only did Ibn Rushd challenge this conception of necessity in the *Tahafut* (cf. Ch.2), but in the commentary on *De caelo* he put forward a very simple table of the modalities envisaged from the point of view of temporality and in the form of opposites.[2]

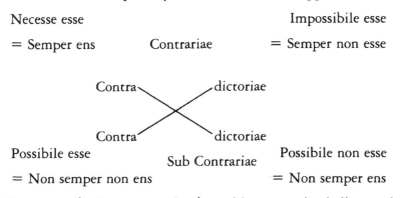

Going even further, not only does this approach challenge the Avicennan perspective, but it most probably provides the key to the whole of Rushdian thought. J. Berque (*Averroes et les contraires*) has drawn attention to the fact that while aligning himself with pre-socratic Hellenism, Ibn Rushd was clearly marked by one of the most characteristic features of Arab culture – namely a sense of ambivalence. This is represented in particular by the linguistic form of *addad* (singular: *didd*) or opposites, which comprise a class of no less than four hundred and twenty six words that can signify opposites (censure – praise; strength – weakness; etc.). Not only does Berque show this feeling of ambivalence in Ibn Rushd's *Fiqh*, in his religious thought and in the philosophical refutation of Ghazali, but he also points out a highly relevant passage in the *Fasl al-maqal* in which Ibn Rushd refers explicitly to the phenomenon of *addad* in order to expose the confusions that can arise from homonyms.

If a single word can indicate different or even opposing things, the only criterion is time. A *didd* only indicates opposites in the dictionary, in reality it indicates one thing at one particular time and another thing at another. The whole of Ibn Rushd's thought consists in shifting from one moment to another. The juridical approach of *ikhtilaf* consists in confronting the practitioner with sometimes equal possibilities between which he must then choose by intuition (*dhawq* – literally 'taste'). However, in theoretical knowledge there are no equivalents, there is what Berque correctly calls 'a gradated theory of truth' (*Averroes et les contraires*, p.139).

The political applications of this will be discussed later. However, it may at once be pointed out that Ibn Rushd was not influenced solely by cultural phenomena and elitist social traditions. The problem is explicitly formulated by him, and in logical terms. Aristotle had already asked whether a notion is logically anterior or posterior to another one which is linked to it (eg.: point – line – surface), or the genus with regard to the species. In the Arab milieu this problem was naturally envisaged in terms of opposites. However, Ibn Sina (perhaps because, despite being an Arabic speaker, he was Indo-European and thought in Persian) rejected the idea that relatives can serve one another as definitions since, he stated, they are simultaneously known but are also simultaneously unknown, and that which is used to explain must be anterior. Ibn Rushd first objected to this in the brief commentary on the *Metaphysics*,[3] saying that a relative, being in essence that which refers to something, cannot be defined without its correlative. This is all the more true since the genus–species hierarchy does not apply in all cases and since it is possibly necessary to find a substitute for the definition.

Here we find a summary of the characteristics of Rushdian thought: breadth of vision and the desire to take the whole of reality into consideration, placing it in hierarchical order but without being exclusive, and the pursuit of solutions as simple as possible, with the imperative that subtlety never led to arbitrary speculation. However, this also constitutes the limitation of this philosophy. While Ibn Rushd might have been able to embrace Hegel's comments on the 'gravity' (*Ernst*) of thought, he could not have gone along with his idea that there is no limit in the search for concepts fitting reality. The resort to temporality is an observation of good sense, which avoids the highly complicated constructions of Ibn Sina, but this temporality is the product of current experience alone – to the extent that when Ibn Rushd's reflections do lead him to perceive a sphere beyond this empirical perspective he is unable to make the leap.

This is indicated on two important points. First, the conception of time itself. In his refutation of Ghazali's critique against the Avicennan conception of eternity, we have seen (Ch.2) that Ibn Rushd implicitly reaches a theory of the ideality of time: 'No motion possesses totality or forms an aggregate, i.e. provided with a beginning or an end, except in so far as it is in the soul, as is the case with time. And it follows from the nature of circular movement that it is neither even nor uneven except as represented in the soul' (*Tahafut*, trans. van den Bergh, vol. I, p.13). However, this Kantian notion of mental time (*dhihni*), although based on a remark made by Aristotle himself according to which 'there can be no time without the soul', is not exploited in itself – any more than it was by the only Arab writer besides Ibn Rushd who managed to perceive it, namely the oriental thinker Abu-l-Barakat al-Baghdadi (died c.560/1164) in whose work it appeared only in a classification.

If Ibn Rushd returns exclusively to the definition of time as 'a number of movements determined by the before and the after', it is in order to confirm that there is no time except when a being in actuality brings into actuality a being in a state of potential, i.e. on the level of particular beings. Here, too, Ibn Rushd who in the face of all scepticism has no doubt that the principle of causality is the basis on which the whole consistency of human knowledge rests, limits himself to testing this causality externally or internally but without daring to make it an *a priori* assumption, like Kant.

THE STATUS OF THE INTELLECT

Anyone trying to understand Ibn Rushd comes up against a major obstacle, namely the amazing variety of levels on which he stands. From the point of view of his own period, he was sometimes the jurist relying on traditional knowledge and at others the religious thinker addressing an enlightened public though of a principally Muslim educational background. Sometimes he was the scientist and sometimes the specialist in a knowledge passed down from Antiquity and, in a sense, esoteric. In his own view there were diverse modes of expression corresponding to the various intellectual levels, although the hierarchy was not totally fixed — sometimes the common people and the philosopher would unite against the dialectician while at others the latter is on an intermediate level between these two. Sometimes the level of expression of the common people is further divided into subsections (poetic or rhetoric). At times he emphasizes the divisions, and at others lingers on one of these levels to define its possibilities envisaged in themselves. Finally, with regard to philosophy in general, he adopts three different perspectives (or perhaps even four including the 'questions') on the work of Aristotle, which is however almost presented as an absolute, and without this corresponding to different audiences.

In studies of the work as a whole, those scholars aspiring to present Ibn Rushd as a philosopher like the others most often simply end up describing a slightly modified Aristotelian system. In such works, the 'philosophy of Averroes' is presented as no more than a blend containing a large portion of Aristotle and a meagre helping of Ibn Rushd. This also prompted Renan to comment that that there was no originality in this thought.

By way of reaction to this, emphasis has been placed on those points where Ibn Rushd affirmed his independence. However, these are often points of detail difficult to co-ordinate by themselves. In the *Encyclopedia of Islam*, R. Arnaldez chose to present only those works known in Arabic, so as to avoid the errors introduced by the translations. Nevertheless, this still does not eliminate the diversity of levels indicated above. This work presents what is primarily an interpretation of Ibn Rushd's *approach*. I am aware that while this may help us understand what he wrote in the context of his own time, it makes it harder to grasp the use to which it might have been put under different circumstances. Ibn Rushd's Latin and Jewish readers were not concerned with him as a person nor even as a thinker. What they wanted from him was instruction, and *solutions*.

Thus it is not possible to evade the essential points which have produced the term 'Averroism', whilst the other commentators

A 'HUMAN' KNOWLEDGE

have not given their name to a school. In the middle ages the following five statements were considered characteristic of this philosophy: (1) The world is eternal; (2) God does not know particulars and there is no Providence; (3) There is no free will; (4) The possible intellect is one numerically, as is the active intellect; hence there is no individual immorality nor individual moral responsibility; (5) Philosophy and theology are contradictory to one another and the supernatural must be rejected.

The fifth point – the 'theory of the double truth' – is simply a distortion from outside of Ibn Rushd's hierarchical conception. Its second aspect, like points (1), (2) and (3), is no more than an extrapolation drawn from the commentaries alone and presented not just as an explanation given on a specific point of Aristotle's work, but as Ibn Rushd's thought itself. Ibn Rushd gives very specific and entirely explicit solutions to points (1) and (2) which we have already examined in detail (see Ch.2). As we have also seen, he gives a somewhat modified response on point (3) but clearly opposes Ibn Tumart's idea of predestination. On the other hand it is more difficult to pronounce on the fourth point, described by Saint Thomas Aquinas as 'the most shameful error' amongst the theses attributed to Ibn Rushd. Readers of 'Averroes' have indeed found in the works translated under this name elements which permit the formulation of this 'technical solution' – which is no longer a simple general position like the theory of the double truth but a response to specific problems which are also not specifically Aristotelian. What is it, then, that leads Ibn Rushd to consider this question, and does his overall approach shed light on the solution he gives – a solution on which, moreover, the specialists are far from being agreed?

As we have seen, the problem of the intellect is from the start so important to Ibn Rushd that he feels the need to explain his own development with regard to it, and his progression from a theory borrowed from Ibn Bajja to a hypothesis of his own (cf. Ch.1). This problem is also present in theological works since it arises in the question of the immortality of the soul. It is certainly no accident that at the time he was writing these works Ibn Rushd also produced some special opuscules in which he took up the questions put forward by Ibn Bajja's work. All these studies were synthesized in the large commentary on *De Anima* just eight years before the author's death.

What stands out most clearly in all these works is the following paradox: J. Jolivet ('Divergences entre les métaphysiques d'Ibn Rushd et d'Aristote') has shown that despite his attempt to purge Aristotle's text of all taint of neoplatonism, Ibn Rushd in fact preserved a part of it:

> The Commentator himself adopts certain modifications (or perhaps they should even be termed developments?) which [the] interpreters [of Aristotle's metaphysics] had subjected it to over the centuries, bringing it closer to its original source, i.e. Platonism. Thus according to Aristotle the heavenly substances were, as a result of their movements, the causes of generation and corruption of the substances of the sublunar world. Ibn Rushd retains this idea but more specifically attributes to the agent Intellect the appearance of forms which continuously succeed one another in matter (p.241), at least the intelligible forms accidentally engendered in individuals. (p. 230 on para. 67 of the brief commentary on *De Anima*)

Not only does he accept the term agent Intellect invented by the commentators but he follows the tradition which likens a concept elaborated from a question of pure noetic in *De Anima* to a cosmological concept found in the *Metaphysics*.

Two not mutually exclusive hypotheses can be formulated to explain his reluctance to restore the true Aristotle. The religious hypothesis is related to the Almohad Profession of faith which insists on the action of divine wisdom in achieving a perfectly ordered world. There are indeed clear Platonic notes in the Mahdi's formula:

> (God) has not ceased and (. . .) will not cease to know all contingencies according to what they represent by their qualities, the details of their genera, the order of their moments and the limit of their numbers; before their being existed the All-Knowing determined it for all eternity; thus they appeared through His wisdom, in conformity with what He determined; thus they came into being through what He determined, following an unshakeable plan and an indestructible organization. (para. II)

However, this does not imply the theory of ideas which, moreover, Ibn Rushd challenges, but simply an activity of thought at the origin of all innovations and modifications in nature:

He did not create them from something that existed eternally with Him; He arranged them with skill, without a model serving as a term of comparison and existing. He produced them as proof of His power and free will; He set them under Him to prove His wisdom and powers of organization. (para. 12)

The scientific hypothesis in turn lays emphasis on Ibn Rushd's need to systematize and the way in which he co-ordinates the observations scattered through the work of Aristotle whilst hardening his positions. It seems he was not satisfied with the brief passage in *De Anima* (III,5) stating: 'in the whole of nature we can distinguish firstly something that serves as matter for each genus (. . .) and then another thing that is the cause and the agent because it produces them all' – a statement inferring that in the soul, besides 'the intellect which is analogous to matter', there must be an intellect which is analogous to the efficient cause.

Ibn Rushd's natural disposition drove him to search the rest of the work, in particular Book XII of the *Metaphysics*, for something to flesh out this comment. Yet at the same time we once again come across the paradox pointed out in the study of the scientific work: in giving priority to overall coherence, Ibn Rushd as a doctor is less 'naturalistic' than Aristotle who *in each field* (the cognitive mechanisms, the causation of beings) followed the logic of observation. The Rushdian synthesis is therefore different from Aristotle's study in that it unifies noetic, metaphysics of causality and astronomy. In Jolivet's view this leads Ibn Rushd to a neoplatonic type of approach:

Situated, by virtue of his imagination (which is corporal) and his contact with the Intellect, between the material world and that of the Intelligences, man's function is to take back forms to their origin by thinking them. This vision is characteristic of neoplatonism, in which the dispersal of the intelligible in the sensible must be compensated for by a reunification and a return to source, of which the agent is none other than the soul.

('Divergences entres les métaphysiques d'Ibn Rushd et d'Aristote', p.242)

However, might this attitude not simply be a result of the influence of the ancient commentators on Ibn Rushd? Why did such a rigorous critic fail to grasp that in this way he was associating himself with a sphere of thought which in other respects he violently opposed? In a word, did this constitute a resurgence of neoplatonism or rather the coincidence of specific theses within two separate perspectives? Jolivet is well aware of this problem, pointing out straight after the remarks cited above that with his affirmation of the identity of the prime substance and the prime mover and the rejection of intermediaries between the unicity of this prime substance and the multiplicity of the world 'Ibn Rushd ceases to be neoplatonic; he returns to Aristotle' (Jolivet, p.244). It is therefore in his theology that we find the reason for his choices in the field of metaphysics.

Yet is there not a contradiction between a theology which affirms the transcendence of God and a metaphysics in which the primary principle, being final and formal causality, 'that which the intelligible exercises on the intellects' (Jolivet, p.244), is simultaneous in the being with the separate substances? Is it not possible to say that 'God is incorporated in the structure of the world?' (Jolivet, p.244).

The first response to this relates to the diversity of levels on which Ibn Rushd stands: theology and metaphysics are not expounded in the same works (although the status of the *Tahafut* is ambiguous), nor are they intended for the same audience. However, this does not completely resolve the question, since it still does not explain why Ibn Rushd agrees in the commentaries to introduce ideas which are clearly alien to Aristotle. If his aim is not to discover the exact philosophical extensions of his theology, what is it?

Ibn Rushd's approach seems to be ruled by the shift from a non-creationist philosophy to a creationist outlook, or in other words by the desire to provide a response to a vital question which Aristotle leaves unresolved: what is the origin of the form received by the matter prepared to receive it? The interpretation given by Almohad theology permits Ibn Rushd to account for the world by hylomorphism, but how is this explanatory framework linked to the image of the Creator put forward by the Mahdi? Ibn Rushd challenges the Platonic interpretation of Themistius who refers back to a being separate from matter — the Soul of the world. In Ibn Rushd's view it is not a question of transmitting something from outside but of bringing into actuality what is in a state of potential:

A 'HUMAN' KNOWLEDGE

(. . .) all forms and the relations between them exist in potential in the prime matter and to an extent in actuality in the Prime Mover which moves the Celestial bodies so that they free precisely those forms that are potential in matter. No immaterial being can act on matter, nor give it form, without using as instruments immutable material beings, i.e. the Heavenly Bodies.

(C. Touati, in *Multiple Averroes*, p.161)

Why then is the Prime Mover conceived in terms of intelligence? There is the Aristotelian model, but for Ibn Rushd this corresponds to a specific need. In the *Tahafut* he has to confront Ghazali's refutation of Ibn Sina's proof of the incorporeality of the Prime Mover. According to Ghazali, the act of accepting the eternity of the world, which is corporeal, must lead on to acceptance of a corporeal principle such as the sun, the supreme heaven or something else. Ibn Rushd considers this to be the reasoning of a *mutakallim* who only introduces differentiation between one thing and its like or its opposite, without taking into account its determination by a wisdom which makes this differentiation necessary in the thing itself. Ibn Rushd thus exactly reiterates the content of Ibn Tumart's formula quoted above, and is well aware of the complete opposition between a doctrine of necessity such as Almohadism and the dialectical arguments of the Ash'arites adopted by Ghazali. Moreover, philosophy concurs with this theory of necessity stemming from a wisdom:

the philosophers (. . .) understand (. . .) by the differentiating principle only that which is determined by the wisdom in the product itself, namely the final cause, for according to them there is no quantity or quality in any being that has not an end based on wisdom, an end which must either be a necessity in the nature of the act of this being or exist in it, based on the principle of superiority.

(*Tahafut*, ed. Bouyges, p.412, trans. van den Bergh, pp.248–9)

Moreover, Aristotle is not the only one involved since, as Ibn Rushd points out, Aristotle had followed Socrates and Plato in praising the theory of Anaxagoras who made the *Intellect* (*Nous*) the Prime Mover. Ibn Tumart had upheld the absolute freedom of God and the idea that there is no finality outside Him, but this finality is still coherent because it is linked to a wisdom which is also creative. While Ibn Rushd exaggerates the similarity between the Almohad creationist theory and the non-creationist theory of the philosophers, he is certainly correct in seeing a greater distance between the Mahdi's doctrine of necessity and the theory of a 'divine custom' (*Sunnat Allah*) which in Ash'arite doctrine reconciles divine free will with the regularity of observed phenomena to the detriment of any coherent causality.

If divine wisdom produces an ordered world, by bringing into actuality potential forms which group concrete individuals into genera and species, so, inversely, through the act of abstraction the human spirit can make these forms exist separately. This is both the most characteristic act of man and that which brings him closest to divinity. While this may legitimately seem to suggest neoplatonism, the preceding discussion demonstrates that it should not necessarily be related to it but rather that it arises from within the Rushdian problematic itself: there is nothing real but the concrete, hence the intelligible being of forms cannot be conceived except as corresponding to a level in the hierarchical structure of existing things where they may have purely intellectual status. Ibn Rushd finds this in the hypothesis of separate intelligences moving the celestial bodies in a manner comparable to the movement of the lover by the loved one, but also of a universal and continuous movement since any individual character could only come from the senses and the imagination which are absent at this level.

Thus the hierarchical structure of the universe and not a mystical type of perspective governs the status of the intellect. The latter, through the simple fact of understanding, i.e. conceptualizing the real, must go back from one intelligible to another towards the organizing wisdom of everything. Consequently, the diverse themes of Providence, the hierarchical structure of the universe and the pivotal role of the human intellect unite in what has come to be called the doctrine of the unity of the intellect. The essential element of this doctrine is the notion of the eternity of the intelligible. To understand this, we have to return right to the very beginning in Aristotle's polemic against both the Megarians and Plato on the question of the appropriateness of conceptual language (universal) to concrete data (particular) (*Metaphysics* 1046, b30). Through this particular aspect, the entire problem of the soundness of thought is advanced. Why do all spirits function in the same way? When the individual stops thinking momentarily or

A 'HUMAN' KNOWLEDGE

definitively, does the truth cease to exist? The Megarians maintain that a concept can only be attributed to an object when the latter demonstrates it in actuality (the architect is only an architect when he actually constructs). Aristotle does not want to bring in the Platonic doctrine of 'participation' in the Idea. He therefore has to invoke the progression of the same being from potential to actuality, and then back to potential, etc. Thus the architect is always an architect from the moment he has learnt his profession, and even when he is not engaged in construction or when he momentarily forgets his skill. The Aristotelian solution is thus to 'expand' experience: momentary contact with the concrete is not enough to justify the attribution of a concept; what is needed is a repetition of this contact, the grasping of a process. If the spirit 'sticks' to this process, there can be no error.

Ibn Rushd simply follows the same logic, extending the analysis to the level of the human species. The individual does not always think the intelligible, but the human species always thinks it, to the extent that Ibn Rushd considers it impossible for it to disappear (Large commentary on *De Anima*, ed. Crawford, p.448). The material intellect, so named because like the prime matter it can change into all things, is always thinking within the activity of the human species − hence the intelligible is eternal. The individual man only loses contact with it through the disappearance of the 'passive powers', i.e. the forms of the imagination, that are corruptible.

The theme of the unity of the intellect was already present in Ibn Bajja's work, but in a completely different context. Ibn Bajja principally describes a 'genesis of thought', whereas in Ibn Rushd's work there is 'a progression to metaphysical analysis' (Jolivet, *Annuaire de l'E.P.H.E.* 1970–1, p.321). This theme enables us to understand not only the 'soundness' of thought, but also, as a result, the philosophical approach advocated by Ibn Rushd. The material intellect reaches perfection (*perfici*) through its own act of understanding material forms, and reaches it to an even greater extent in turning to immaterial forms 'intelligible in themselves', in particular the agent Intellect. Thus it reaches the level of the eternity of thought (ed. Crawford, p.450). The term 'union' or 'conjunction' (*ittisal, continuatio*) to the agent Intellect is used to describe the process by which the material intellect, which is nothing in actuality, becomes what it thinks and is united with the intelligible. It assumes a preparation involving the gradual acquisition of science, although the end of this process is itself beyond speculative science.

The details of the Rushdian concept of the intellect are extremely complex, and Renan himself was appalled by them. In fact, as mentioned, Ibn Rushd generally looks for the simplest solutions, since he considers complexity a source of error. However, on this particular problem he had to deal with an essential point on which the layers of commentaries and hypotheses had accumulated without it being possible to draw a clear opposition between the perspectives because, as J. Jolivet correctly points out, Aristotle's own perspective is tinged with Platonism. If Ibn Rushd's solution has been seen as neoplatonic in tone, it is because he wishes to take into account all the interpretations and do justice to each one, not through syncretism, but by integrating the particular aspect that justified its formulation.

He distinguishes thought, which is passive, from abstraction, which is active and anterior to the former in our will. We understand the 'primary propositions' (*primae propositiones*) in a natural way through the action of the agent Intellect, and 'knowledge acquired (*intellecta acquisita*) from the primary propositions' in voluntary fashion both from the former and from the agent Intellect. The agent Intellect acts towards these primary propositions in a manner analogous to the cause efficient in relation to the instrument, or form in relation to matter, but this manner remains autonomous. This explains the capacity of the material intellect to grasp eternally both material forms and separate forms. In 'engendering' intelligibles, which is an action of the material intellect, but assumes the intervention of the agent Intellect, the latter becomes a form of the former. This is what constitutes union, but it takes place through a whole series of mediations: material intellect – images – potential speculative intelligibles – speculative intelligibles in actuality – agent Intellect. The Latin text (which is the only one known) speaks of 'movement towards junction' (*moveri ad continuationem*, p.500) and shows how Ibn Rushd was attracted – but not more than attracted – by the mystical perspective of Themistius.

The treatise *De animae beatitudine* goes into even greater detail concerning the action of the agent Intellect. Since it renders material forms intelligible, it must be superior to them in intelligibility and there must be a mediator – the acquired intellect, which is that which is capable of thinking itself and which develops in time. The *intellectus–intellectio*, the *intelligibile* and the *intelligens* are thus united in a quasi religious perspective.

THE HUMAN COMMUNITY AND THE POLITICAL COMMUNITY

Despite the fact that Ibn Rushd had no important followers in the Muslim circles, that his work only survived thanks to his influence on a certain Jewish bourgeoisie, and finally that his philosophy has become famous through its distorted presentation in a heterodox Aristotelianism arising from a specifically Parisian milieu – all this does not mean we can consider him a marginal figure in his own world. It is important not to judge on the basis of subsequent events, since the crisis of Almohadism, closely followed by the decisive advance of the Christians into Spain, destroyed all the normal conditions for the diffusion of a doctrine. Rather, he should be compared to those who came before him. Ibn Rushd was the first and only philosopher in the Muslim West to gain status in legal circles as well as an audience that extended beyond doctrinal divisions and was almost as important amongst his contemporaries as Ibn al-Mujahid who dominated the sphere of mysticism. This status and this audience were primarily the result of his work as a jurist – and this in itself was a great novelty in the field of *Falsafa*. However, he also owed them to his interpretation of ideology in power which, like his juridical works, was supported by his official functions.

This position also had its drawbacks. Breaking new ground in an environment that was intellectually unprepared, Ibn Rushd had to build up an audience. His own society did not recognise the status of the philosopher, acknowledging only that of the scholar or the politician (*faqih* or counsellor to the prince). These two figures were permitted – within the limits of orthodoxy – to construct their own vision of the world although, whatever its merit, it did not endow them with any moral authority. Such authority only existed in the ancient world. To gain an audience, the thinker had to turn himself into a scholar of the philosophical 'tradition'. Malik Ibn Wuhayb's success in this respect – despite his failure to produce anything of his own – earned him the title of 'philosopher of the Occident' amongst his contemporaries. If Ibn Rushd goes so far as to subject himself to the discipline of the commentary which is not only detailed but coherent, it is because he saw the principal danger to lie in the temptations of syncretism.

Above all, he had a very humble conception of his role as a philosopher, as Ibn Sab'in was later to confirm, despite his stern attitude towards Ibn Rushd. Ibn Rushd believed that wisdom transcends individuals. The wise man finds happiness in being the subject in which it is momentarily realized. Ibn Bajja had declared that the union of the human intellect with the agent Intellect is possible and that this is where supreme happiness lies. Knowledge of separate substances denied in certain texts, notably al-Farabi, is attained if the quiddity of the intelligibles is individualized in the act of recognition and is multiplied in accordance with the different thinking subjects. Ibn Rushd objects that it is not possible to talk in the same way about the quiddity of material things and the quiddity of intelligible things. Furthermore, Ibn Bajja believes that the material intellect is subject to generation and corruption, which makes it impossible for it to think the incorruptible; and in conceding that it is not subject to it and thinks eternally, this makes it impossible for intellection to take place within a determined time. Ibn Rushd's solution is to state that the material intellect is eternal and belongs not to each corruptible individual but to the whole of the human species — which like all species is eternal (as a corollary of the Aristotelian doctrine of the eternity of the world). This material intellect is able both to conceive material forms, hence the existence within it of ideas subject to evolution, and separate forms, which permits union with the agent Intellect which forms these intelligibles. Speculative knowledge, with which individuals can help one another through a process of accumulation, prepares the way for this final knowledge which in turn transcends it since it is no longer dependent on sensible experience.

In contrast to the haughty isolation of the mystics and the advocates of illumination like Ibn Tufayl or Ibn Bajja's 'solitaries', the process by which philosophy is carried out is, according to Ibn Rushd, the concern of humanity as a whole. Both are eternal, and philosophy must always be being enacted in one part of the world or another. On the other hand, any personal elements in the thought of the individual spring from the imagination and are therefore perishable.

This keen awareness of the insignificance of man and the greatness of thought is a continuation of the doctrine of the Mahdi described by the traditionalists as 'the doctrine of the Logos'. It was violently repudiated in the period of tension resulting from the problems of the Almohad regime and from the Christian threat. In the panic that set in well before the towns actually fell one after the other, the men of religion were far more attracted to a legalism which favoured accommodation and the search for the 'best', and to a mysticism giving precedence to the individual endowed with supernatural powers.

In short, the men of religion like the philosophers before Ibn Rushd, failed to combine a personal perspective with a concern for the public good. Ibn Rushd's approach was more balanced. Unlike Ibn Bajja he did not play the role of counsellor, nor did he compose a wholly circumstantial work like Ibn Tufayl. Instead he applied himself to the commentaries on Aristotle's *Nichomachean Ethics* and particularly, in the absence of Aristotle's *Politics*, to that on Plato's *Republic*. However, these commentaries are not just scholarly exercises and, while the commentary on the *Ethics* is strictly theoretical, there is frequent reference to the current state of affairs in that on the *Republic*. Most of the Arabic version of the commentary on the *Ethics* has now been lost, but it has been preserved in Hebrew and Latin translation. The work is a middle commentary and thus Ibn Rushd does not simply expound Aristotle's thought, but expresses himself freely and introduces explanations and examples of his own. The work deals with the first part of political science, 'customs and volitional actions, and behaviour' in general. The *Republic* shows 'how these customs are established in souls'. This last commentary, which has been completely lost in Arabic, is nevertheless well known today in the Hebrew translation. It too is a middle commentary, although in certain respects it is also a brief commentary since Ibn Rushd does not take into consideration the first book, most of the second, the tenth, and parts of books III–IX of the original work, claiming that he is only interested in demonstrative arguments and that these passages only contain dialectical ones. Similarly, he supplements Plato with ideas and formulae borrowed from Aristotle, particularly the *Nichomachean Ethics*, and makes theoretical digressions on psychology and epistemology based on Aristotle. Almost two thirds of the work is made up of comments and explanations.

His approach can be seen as a continuation of al-Farabi who had dealt with the two ancient thinkers in a similar way. Unlike his predecessor, Ibn Rushd does not attempt to reconcile the two at all costs, and he is generally aware of the differences between Plato and Aristotle. However, in the discussion of politics, he rarely opposes the two. Al-Farabi also serves as model for the way in which he envisages the links between this political philosophy and religious Law, particularly Islamic *Shari'a*. However, he is more conscious than al-Farabi of the supremacy of the *Shari'a* – a fact explained by his position as a jurist and by the climate of Almohadism. He generally accepts the basic conclusions of Plato's politics, though corrected by Aristotle, and considers synthesis not just applicable (whereas for Plato this would require almost impossible conditions) but applicable to his own society as long as enlightened leaders succeed one another.

Ibn Rushd's defence of philosophy, which distinguishes him as a thinker from the other ulema, may even be seen as an adaptation to Islamic norms of the Platonic requirement that government be just in its beliefs and convictions. However, the political situation of his own time features in his formulation of this doctrine which is both Islamic and Platonic. Defining injustice as a situation in which 'each of the citizens prospers by means of more than one occupation', he adds, 'as happens in our country'. He envisages the ideal city and its degeneration as described by Plato, and opposes the Golden Age of the Prophet and his successors to the later Muslim states which, while theoretically maintaining the ideal structure and constitutional practices of early Islam, are in fact a distortion of it.

Some of the references are very precise, as in the description of the decline of the Almoravid regime:

> In the beginning they imitated the constitution based on the Law – this was the case under the first of them. Then under his son this changed to a timocratic regime, since it was combined with a love of money. Later, his grandson changed this into a hedonistic regime with all the characteristics of hedonism, and it perished during his time. The reason for this is that the regime which opposed it (Almohadism) resembled the regime based on the Law.
>
> (ed. Rosenthal, pp.227 and 292)

Similarly, he specifically mentions the tale of Ibn Ghanya, the last Almoravid governor of Cordoba, in order to illustrate the shift from democracy to tyranny.

A 'HUMAN' KNOWLEDGE

His support for the Almohad regime is not only indicated by these judgements on recent history. Certain philosophical theses are also slanted towards its ideology. Al-Farabi had already presented Aristotle as being in disagreement with Plato's thesis on the wars of the virtuous city and its extent, but in agreement with Islamic Law. While Plato sees the origin and aim of the war as the desire for greater luxury, entailing the extension of the city, Ibn Rushd does not follow the order of the text under commentary and refuses to discuss the temperament of the soldiers and the virtue of the irascible soul, i.e. courage. Instead he replaces it with an explanation of the means by which courage and the other practical virtues are acquired. One of these means is constraint: in the virtuous city its application is limited to training for the art of war, but externally it serves to spread virtue amongst other nations, with the virtuous city acting as the father of the family and keeping the troublesome nations under its guardianship for the period needed for their education. While Plato states that the courage of the virtuous city is developed in order to carry out its own activities or for wars undertaken through necessity, in Ibn Rushd's view it is developed principally for war and cannot be realized if war is not continuous. This comes close to a problem already implicitly raised in the *Bidaya*. In its initial draft this juridical treatise ignored the duty of the pilgrimage in accordance with a Spanish tradition adopted by the Almohads who viewed Holy War as the ultimate duty. In his final draft, just before the chapter on Holy War, Ibn Rushd adds another chapter on the pilgrimage, since the idea of it spread once the Almohads aspired to extend their rule as far as Arabia. If this seems to follow the traditional structure of Malikite and Andalusian treatises, placing Holy War just after the acts of worship, it is purely a result of the practical coincidence between the geographical directions of the two duties in question.

Conversely, when Plato puts forward a more radical idea, Ibn Rushd delights in his radicalism and is moved to oppose not only the moderation of Aristotle but even Muslim custom. This is true, for example, on the question of the equality of the sexes regarding civic duties. Ibn Rushd criticises the Islamic tradition which only takes women into consideration in their reproductive role. Whilst Ibn Sina, who in other respects is much closer to Platonism, reiterates the strict laws concerning the necessary seclusion of women and their material dependence on their husband, Ibn

Rushd condemns this enforced uselessness and sees it as 'one of the causes of the poverty of these states'.

To an extent the political thought is a synthesis of Ibn Rushd's diverse investigations. He sees the common people as the recipient of rhetorical arguments aiming initially to instil adherence to sound beliefs and later to achieving good behaviour. Whereas Aristotle (*Nichomachean Ethics* 1179 a–b) considered it impossible to achieve the latter through argument alone, we have seen how Ibn Rushd benefited from analysis of the Almohad propaganda methods to challenge his master on the subject of the citizens. With regards to enemies, the use of coercion is necessary, and on this point Ibn Rushd challenges Plato who only envisages war against the Barbarians and merely 'fraternal reprimands' amongst the Greeks: there are various levels of virtue even within the community based upon sound opinions, as Ibn Tumart's *tamyiz* taught. This is revealed in the practice of war which supposes an apprenticeship to discipline and, as already stated, this must be continuous since the exercise of the virtue of courage requires continuous conflict.

For the 'guardians of the city' this conflict extends onto the intellectual level. Summoned to become leaders, they must struggle against the persuasive arguments that have shaped them initially, in order to raise themselves to the level of demonstrative arguments. There is thus a gradation starting with poetic arguments which aim solely at imitation even if this is false – as in certain children's fables – then rhetorical arguments which give possible imitation, dialectical arguments giving correct imitation, and finally demonstrative arguments, reserved for the elite, which are the only ones that give reality and above all lead to the truth.

The shift from dialectical arguments to demonstrative argumentation is represented in particular by the criticism of the atomist theory of the Mutakallimun, a theory intended to prove that there is no efficacy except in God. Besides the theoretical consequence that there must then be a principle of evil, Ibn Rushd draws from this the practical conclusion that there is no stability of good and evil. It is not only necessary to reject fables promising punishment or reward, which only incite action if the reward appears adequate or the fear is enough to act as a deterrent; it is also necessary to reject everything that prevents a grasp of that which is specific to each being. Classification by genus and species is the only method that enables the world to be put in order, or at least most of it,

A 'HUMAN' KNOWLEDGE

and it is naturally re-enacted in the political divisions which must be clear and unambiguous so as to avoid the risk of disorder. Dialectical argument is doubtless superior to poetical or rhetorical argument, but it is more perilous as it can lead to deception if it becomes sophistical. In presenting itself as exclusive and unsurpassable it leads to the fragmentation of the collectivity. The Platonic affirmation of the need for a stable form of knowledge in order to safeguard a common language and thus a social community is clearly at the root of Ibn Rushd's thought. Hence the third part of the commentary on the *Republic* gives a lengthy description of the different forms of social degeneration.

This work can thus correctly be described as a 'pedagogical treatise'. Because it relies on the objectivity of ethics, politics becomes the basis for the entire edifice of commentaries designed to provide an ideal picture of human knowledge. It in turn is guided by the model provided by theological reflection, making it possible for each person to achieve happiness according to his own capabilities, and through its main conclusions. Finally, like Plato, Ibn Rushd compares the acts of the political leader to those of the doctor. We have seen in the discussion of the *Kulliyat* how he envisages the latter: the doctor acts in accordance with each case, but bearing in mind the order of nature, and in a manner that reconciles the one with the other following a procedure governed by the laws of the discovery of the truth.

4

AN AMBIGUOUS AUDIENCE

THE MUSLIM MILIEU

Ibn Rushd is a paradoxical figure in the history of the Islamic world. It was he, in person, who succeeded in bringing philosophy out of the ghetto to which it had been confined. Yet his work was not continued after his death. This paradox merits further consideration.

Ibn Rushd's juridical works set him apart from the other *Falasifa*. While the latter often played a political role as ministers or counsellors to the ruler, their influence was limited to very narrow circles and they had little impact on the real life of the populace. Ibn Rushd, on the other hand, was a Qadi and came into contact with the people and their daily problems. If he suffered humiliations at the hands of the masses, it was because he accepted such contact. In addition his juridical work prepared for, and to an extent shaped, a theologico-philosophical work directly linked to the ideology of the time. All this resulted in a considerable audience which placed him, if not amongst the leading group of scholars of the period, at least in fourteenth place, which meant that he was still amongst those masters with an appreciable audience.

Yet he remains an isolated figure. Like several other contemporary scholars even more eminent than he, Ibn Rushd did not manage to become incorporated into an educational system (see *Le Monde des ulemas andalous*, pp.178–9). This can be blamed on the fact that he worked during a transitional period when force of circumstances meant that several prominent individuals were left on their own, whereas the structure of the preceding and following periods was more all-embracing. His elitist ideology doubtless also

AN AMBIGUOUS AUDIENCE

played a part, despite all his attempts to affirm that it was meant to co-exist harmoniously with the popular sensibility.

However, even his known disciples did not propagate his philosophy – including those who could have left some productive trace of it. This was the case with Abu Muhammad Ibn Hawt Allah, whose conciliatory attitude towards pre-existing trends was ultimately preferred by the Almohad rulers to the intellectual rigours of Ibn Rushd. Working in Majorca, he crystallized the confrontation between Zahirite *fiqh* and Ash'arite Kalam and prepared the ground for the emergence of Ramon Lull's work.[1] However, as we shall see, Lull completely misunderstood the true meaning of Ibn Rushd's thought and referred only to Latin Averroism in order to challenge it.

The behaviour of the proponents of philosophy had greater impact, since it obscured Ibn Rushd's work without leaving it even a marginal influence. It appears that the logician Ibn Tumlus of Alcira was a disciple of Ibn Rushd's but – perhaps as a result of Ibn Rushd's disgrace – he never quoted him but openly drew on al-Farabi. This might be excusable had he not, in the historical introduction to his work, given an enthusiastic airing to the confusion between Almohadism and the teachings of Ghazali, despite all Ibn Rushd's efforts to avoid this. It is, however, true that he did not go beyond the level of logical technique, on which the doctrinal consequences of this confusion did not emerge.[2]

This does not mean Ibn Rushd could have been saved by the speculative thinkers. There is a famous declaration of his taken from Socrates: 'Oh men! I do not say that this science that you call divine science is false, but I do say that I myself am knowledgeable in human science.' Such words can only have alienated him from those who, in the confusion brought about by the disintegration of the Almohad system and the collapse of Muslim power in the face of the Christians, sought safety in mystical escape, which redoubled their flight towards the East. The attitude of the two chief Andalusian representatives of this trend is symptomatic.

On the one hand is Ibn Sab'in who wished, however, to provide a philosophical basis for his mystical experience, and produced a long-lasting and distorted picture of Ibn Rushd's attitude to Aristotle:

This man, Ibn Rushd, was seduced by Aristotle and

dedicated himself to his glorification. He imitates him, not only in his perceptions but in his basic ways of thought. If he had been told that Aristotle said someone was standing and sitting at the same time, he would have said and believed this. The majority of his works are taken from Aristotle's teaching, be it in his commentaries on him or the way he follows his line of thinking. In himself, he was a man of limited scope, faint understanding, foolish conceptions and lacking in intuition. Yet he was a fine man — discreet, equitable and aware of his failings. We cannot speak of his personal work, since he was merely an imitator of Aristotle.[3]

As for Ibn 'Arabi, the greatest name in theosophy, the account he gives of an interview he had with Ibn Rushd during his youth aims simply to destroy the philosopher's image and present him as entertaining doubts regarding his entire work. First, it should be pointed out that Ibn 'Arabi was in conflict with the whole world of Almohadism. This is revealed by an allusion to a discussion he had with the Sultan Ya'qub al-Mansur. Although the latter had just exiled Ibn Rushd, he does not seem to have let himself be impressed by the supernatural gifts in front of which Ibn 'Arabi was used to seeing the world bow down, since Ibn 'Arabi complained that he had abased his reputation. He also opposed Abu Abd Allah b. Jabir (also called Ibn Junayd) of Cabrafigo near Ronda, whom he described as a 'mu'tazilite sufi'. This term should not be taken to mean that he belonged to this school, which may not have had any followers in Spain except under the Umayyad caliphate. Most probably, it implies that he followed in the line of Ibn Tufayl, combining belief in illumination with belief in the Almohad doctrine of the divine attributes. This is very close to the position of the Kharijis who were in turn strongly influenced by Mu'tazilism. From the denial of the possibility of understanding the attributes in God and in man in the same way, Ibn Jabir goes against Ibn 'Arabi to conclude that the believer is incapable of imitating a divine attribute.

The passage concerning Ibn Rushd, which is told in a conceited tone characteristic of Ibn 'Arabi, describes a scene that must have taken place around 580/1184, two years after Ibn Rushd left his post as Qadi of Seville to become Qadi of Cordoba. Having kept in contact with his former fellow-citizens, Ibn Rushd heard about the path recently taken by the young Ibn 'Arabi. There is nothing to contradict the authenticity of this meeting, which can be explained by the curiosity of the philosopher and perhaps even more by his desire to find out about what he was up against. It is true that politeness towards a friend's son may have prevented Ibn Rushd from being quite so categorical in his rejection as the Almohad Sultan was later to be. Yet it is impossible to believe the version given by Ibn 'Arabi which constitutes a denial of Ibn Rushd's work:

> Upon my entrance the philosopher got up and came to meet me with numerous gestures of friendship and respect, and finally embraced me. Then he said: 'Yes'. And I in turn said to him: 'Yes'. At this point his joy increased on seeing that I had understood him. But then realising what had provoked his joy, I said: 'No'. Immediately Ibn Rushd grew tense. The colour of his features changed and he seemed to doubt what he was thinking. He questioned me: 'What kind of solution have you found through illumination and divine inspiration? Is it identical to that given to us by speculative reflection?' I replied: 'Yes and no. Between the yes and the no spirits take flight outside their matter and necks detach themselves from their bodies.' Ibn Rushd grew pale and I saw him tremble. He murmured the ritual phrase: 'There is no strength but in God', for he had understood what I was referring to (. . .). I have been told that he gave thanks to God for having made him live at a time when he could see someone who had entered into spiritual retreat as an ignorant man and emerge from it as I had. 'This is an example,' he said, 'the possibility of which I had affirmed myself, but without ever having met anyone who had actually experienced it. Glory be to God who made me live at a time when one of the masters of this experience lives, a man who can unlock His gates. Glory be to God who did me the personal favour of seeing one of these men with my own eyes.'[4]

The beginning of the conversation, with all its unspoken innuendos, is the product of a thought that recognises telepathy as a form of communication. It is inconceivable coming from the mouth of a man who at the time was working on a detailed, rational commentary on Aristotle's work. Such anxiety over the agreement of reason and illumination makes no sense in a thinker who reproached Ibn Tufayl for adding extra-rational elements to philosophy. Finally, the assurance given by a master of philosophy of the possibility of mystical experience almost instantaneously transforming an ignorant man into an *'arif* (initiate) contradicts the critique of Sufism as a cause of spiritual unrest.

If Ibn 'Arabi reinterprets the scene in his own favour, it is because this enables him to place rational thought on a lower plane in his mental universe. In this way he could eliminate any difficulties likely to arise from a confrontation with rational thought by appealing to something beyond it, which even its greatest representatives supposedly acknowledged. This explains his symbolic interpretation of Ibn Rushd's funeral which he attended and where he noted that the body was transported on an animal whose load was balanced by his philosophy books: 'A bundle of books balancing a corpse!'

Suffering from the disappearance of the Almohad doctrine to which he had wished to contribute, caught between the various forms of voluntary ignorance, contempt and misrepresentation, Ibn Rushd saw his thought disappear from the Muslim scene. In the course of his innumerable readings, H. Corbin finds no references to him whatsoever in Eastern works, except in Lahiji (eleventh/ seventeenth century) who mistakenly calls him Ibn Rashid (*Multiple Averroes*, pp. 324–5). However, in the middle of the nineteenth century, the publishing efforts of the German orientalist Muller very quickly stimulated similar works in the Arab World. In the course of the Renaissance (*Nahda*), Ibn Rushd was rediscovered as a forerunner of modern thought – initially in a manner similar to Renan, and later taking into account the modifications introduced by criticism.

In practice, this rediscovery was partially twisted by external factors. The most famous of the rehabilitators of Ibn Rushd is Farah Antun (1874–1922), a Christian of Lebanese origin who settled in Egypt where he worked as an editor, having previously spent time in America. In his essay *Ibn Rushd wa falsafatuhu* (Ibn Rushd and his philosophy) which first appeared in the journal *Al-Jami'a* and was then published separately in Cairo in 1903, he took up Renan's thesis that Islam had destroyed the philosophical spirit in Ibn Rushd. The conflict between science and religion can be resolved as long as each is fundamentally separated from the other, since the former springs from the intellect and the latter from the heart, and each has its specific methods and applications – observation and experience on the one hand, and on the other fideist acceptance of the Revelation with the aim of recognising virtues and vices and the world beyond.

Imbued with the secular ideology of the West which he openly aspired to introduce into the East, Antun certainly did not believe that his own religion would have behaved better than Islam towards Ibn Rushd. However, Muhammad 'Abduh, leader of the Muslim reformists, believed, or at least pretended to believe, that this was his ulterior motive. Ibn Rushd thus became the pretext for a polemic that had little to do with him. While Abduh elaborated his attacks on Christianity which were to culminate in his famous work *Al-Islam wa-l-Nasraniya* (Islam and Christianity) which appeared in Cairo in 1367/1947–8, Antun set out his social and political views in his journals. Antun's aim was not in fact to affirm the superiority of one religion over another but, rather the opposite, to establish a system in which all religions would be equal – a system founded on the basic principles of humanity, of which the positive religions only present accidental developments. He has no hesitation in referring to the old concept of allegorical interpretation (*ta'wil*) to show that concrete precepts have no aim other than the development of general virtue. On these last points, as we can see, he is not far from his model.

Moreover, Muhammed Abduh's misinterpretation is not directed against Ibn Rushd as such. In a way, the reformist movement can sometimes draw upon his teachings. This has been demonstrated, for example, on several occasions by the current Algerian government which appeals to the reformist approach of Ibn Badis. Indeed, this author is himself a privileged witness to the fluctuations of official intentions as a result of far more concrete imperatives. Rushdian tones can be heard issuing from the mouths of many contemporary Arab intellectuals, above all in the context of official ceremonies and amongst people of the same milieu (for example, the conference of Kairouan 23–7 March 1975: *Al-'ilm wa-l-iman fi-l-Islam* (Science and faith in Islam), Tunis, Ministry for Cultural Affairs 1395/1975). It is unlikely that such statements of intention go beyond these circles of initiates. On the other hand, with the current rise of fundamentalism, it is not unusual to hear other intellectuals attack Ibn Rushd by brazenly adopting the insulting title of *mutafalsif* which he had to endure during his disgrace.

In India the particular situation which enabled the emergence of tendencies aiming to oppose Western colonization with its own weapons also favoured the acquisition of real authority for Rushdian thought, not so much as the glory of Islam in general as for its rationalism which was capable of providing a new foundation for the Muslim religion. This was the work of Sir Sayyid Ahmad Khan (1815–98) in Aligarh and above all of Amir Ali (1849–1928) in Bengal. However, there too – although for other reasons (essentially the influence of the puritanical wahhabis on the moderate Hanafi attitudes of the Indian Muslims, coinciding with a similar climate within Hinduism that produced the conservative teachings of Ramakrishna and Vivekananda) – the idea of undertaking personal reflection was eventually judged harshly by the public who regarded it as an elitist attitude taken by the intellectual classes.

THE JEWISH MILIEU

Arabic, the language of culture for Muslims familiar with the phenomenon of diglossia – classical Arabic/spoken language (dialectal Arabic, Berber or Romance) – also imposed itself as such on non-Muslims. The 'mozarabs', or 'Arabized' Christians lacked the vitality to develop a genuinely philosophical system of thought, despite the preliminary work of Bishops Recemundo and Abu-l-Harith in the fourth/tenth century. In the period under consideration they were suspected of collusion with the princes in the north of the peninsula who were displaying their hostility. As a result, the Christians were obliged either to join the princes, or emigrate to North Africa, where like those who stayed behind they were eventually absorbed into the Muslim population.

The Jews on the the other hand did not pose a threat. Despite various outbursts of hostility against them as a result of the important political posts held by some, they were able to develop their own culture. However, their relationship with the Arabic language was ambiguous. Their common membership of the semitic world served as a stepping-stone that enabled them to build up a highy developed field of linguistic scholarship and also a fairly creditable imitative literature. However, this kind of proximity was also dangerous, and by the fifth/eleventh century onwards half the Andalusian Jews had lost the use of Hebrew. All the major works were composed in Arabic so as to be understood, including those of purely Jewish relevance such as Ha-Levi's *Kuzari*. Conversely, as the Jews began to suffer the persecutions of the

Almohad regime and forced conversions, they reverted to Hebrew in the course of their emigration to the East and particularly towards Christian Europe, and those who went to Europe lost the habitual use of Arabic.

It was thanks to this process that Ibn Rushd's work, which was ignored in its own milieu, passed to the West, where, once immediate contact with Arabic had been lost, it began to be translated into Hebrew starting in 1232.

Was this Jewish audience the result of Ibn Rushd's forced stay in Lucena? It is true that in these surroundings Averroean rationalism found a terrain prepared by another form of more specifically Jewish rationalism, the most famous expression of which is the work of Ibn Maymun (Maimonides 1135–1204). Despite medieval tales describing the friendly relationship between the two philosophers, Muslim and Jew, Ibn Maymun only declared himself to be a disciple of a pupil of Ibn Bajja and it was not until his exile in Egypt that he read some of Ibn Rushd's commentaries.

His Aristotelianism did not bring the same rupture as that introduced by Ibn Rushd into Muslim thought. For him, the Almohad background constituted a framework – one provided by his enforced Islamic studies – but one which remained external. His major work, the 'guide of the perplexed' (*Dalalat al-ha'irin*) exactly followed many aspects of the thought of Ibn Bajja, whose break with neoplatonism was far less radical than that of Ibn Rushd. It is even quite possible that in the section that differentiates him most strongly from Ibn Rushd – i.e. his determination of the limits of human knowledge which is incapable of knowing God and the separate substances – he goes back to some texts of al-Farabi which are only indirectly known to us. Finally, he comes close to the Avicennism of Ibn Tufayl in juxtaposing a strictly deductive method in the details of the analysis with the conception of metaphysical knowledge as illumination, but without revealing the link between the two.

Nevertheless, Ibn Maymun claimed to appeal to reason alone and not to be the upholder of any metaphysical tradition. Aristotle is considered the supreme authority with regard to the sublunar world but beyond this his thought is only conjectural. The assumption that governs the accord between philosophy and religion is that in the field of physics (in the account of the creation) and metaphysics (in the initial vision of Ezekiel) the Scripture and tradition contain what is found to be true by the philosophers, notably Aristotle. It is therefore necessary both to interpret these texts so as to weed out anything that would be impious if taken literally and to eliminate fruitless and harmful approaches, particularly Kalam, as with Ibn Rushd, but also philosophy if it surpasses the sublunar sphere. Like the Muslim thinker, Ibn Maymun considers it necessary to talk to the common people by means of images, but he is prepared to reveal many more of the real meanings to them. Rather than specifying what philosophy has to say, he sets about eliminating its apparent contradiction with religion by distinguishing the various levels of meaning within it according to the method of Aristotle and al-Farabi: literal – figurative, univocal – equivocal, etc.

Despite these divergences, an authentic Jewish 'Averroism' started to appear with the generation of Ibn Maymun's disciples. Mixing Ibn Rushd and Ibn Sina it was later to give rise to the theory of the 'double truth'. Ibn Rushd's text itself was preserved by the Jewish writers in three different forms – Arabic, Arabic written in Hebrew script, and Hebrew translation. This was a result of the very close communications and rapid interaction between the communities of Spain and those of Provence-Languedoc.

The main reason for the interest in these texts is doubtless the sharpness of the distinctions between Ibn Rushd and Ibn Sina, since Ibn Maymun is frequently much closer to the latter. While Moses ben Joseph Ha-Levi of Seville prefers Ibn Sina, the Catalan or Provençal Isaac Albalag (second half of the thirteenth century) draws mainly on Ibn Rushd in order to criticise the presentation of Ibn Sina made by Ghazali as a prelude to the refutation of him he was to undertake. G. Vajda who made a study of Albalag,[5] believes that this convinced rationalist must have been influenced by Latin Averroism, possibly via the apostate Abner of Burgos. Albalag does not, however, accept the thesis according to which there is complete fusion of the human intellect with the separate intelligences after the purification of physical death. He is joined in his opinion by the Italian writer Hillel ben Samuel of Verona who, in his criticism of Ibn Rushd on this point, simply adopts the analyses of Saint Thomas Aquinas. Hence Judaism was not simply an intermediary between Ibn Rushd and the Scholastics through the translations. There were also interferences and counter-influences.

It was above all in the French Midi that the vitality of Jewish thought manifested itself. The communities of the region were affected by two polemics: one which arose around 1230 and involved a confrontation between supporters and opponents of Maimonides, and the other which took place in 1303–6 at which time Maimonides' authority was no longer challenged although philosophical and scientific studies were still in question. In particular there were complaints at the spectacle of 'men burying themselves in (. . .) the books of Ibn Rushd'.[6] Once the crisis had pa. 3ed and the triumph of rationalism was assured, it is no exaggeration to say that the influence of Ibn Rushd equalled that of Maimonides. The two were now the great masters of Jewish thought. Yet despite the fact that Maimonides remained the object of deep veneration and despite the stream of praises heaped upon him, in certain remarks it is possible to detect regret that the great Jewish theologian should have adopted the basic positions of al-Farabi and Ibn Sina while failing to take into consideration those of his great Arab contemporary and countryman. Jewish thought in the south of France came to adopt all the criticisms levelled by Averroes at the theses of Avicenna: his distinction between essence and existence was rejected; his principle 'From the One comes only the one' was denied; the soul he had attributed to the Celestial Spheres in addition to their intellect was ruled out; the Alfarabo-Avicennan schema concerning the procession of the Intellects and the Celestial Spheres, which had been the target of the mockery of Ghazali and Juda Ha-Levi, was abandoned, etc.. Subjects barely touched upon by the *Guide of the Perplexed*, such as noetics and the immortality of the soul, assumed great importance because Averroes had dealt with them so fully. He had completely renewed the question of prophecy. His extensive criticism of the idea of the temporal creation of the world forced reconsideration of the question that Maimonides had been incapable of resolving in a purely rational way. The solution given by Maimonides to the problem of divine omniscience seemed unsatisfactory. Finally, his two apparently irreconcilable theories on Providence had only perplexed his readers. (Ch. Tonati)[7]

The work of the mathematician, philosopher and theologian Levi ben Gershon (Gersonides) (1288–1344) is important in this context. While he never displays servility towards Arab philosophy, he nevertheless draws upon it extensively. He was in contact with the Christian intellectuals and knew something of their culture, though not in the Latin texts and only through oral

Provençal translations. On the other hand, he did know a little Arabic which was enough for him to make use of the technical comments on Ibn Rushd's texts given by the Arabists, but not enough for him to deal directly with the works which he quotes only in translation. He did not know the theological works or the *Tahafut* (though it was translated during his lifetime), but he was familiar with the large commentary on the *Metaphysics* and the middle commentaries on *De anima, De caelo, De generatione et corruptione, Meteorologies, Nichomachean Ethics* and Plato's *Republic*. Between 1321 and 1324 he produced his own commentaries on the middle commentaries on the *Physics* and the whole of the *Organon*, and the brief commentaries on the *Physics, De generatione et corruptione, Meteorologies, De anima, De partibus* and *De generatione animalium*, and *Parva Naturalia*. He also made a commentary on the *Treatise on the conjunction with the Agent Intellect*. Finally, in the *book of the sane syllogism* (1319) he attempted to correct the errors of Aristotle that had been transmitted by Ibn Rushd.

He does not rely solely on the texts since he claims to have verified everything Ibn Rushd said on the subject of plants. However, he reacts in the same way as Ibn Rushd when confronted with Aristotle's errors, which he tends to attribute to copyists' mistakes in view of the depth of the Master's thought. With regards to the form of the commentary, he deals with Ibn Rushd in the same way as Ibn Rushd dealt with Aristotle, using simple paraphrase interspersed with objections followed by proposed solutions, all in accordance with purely rational criteria. The problem of the relationship between philosophy and religion is only broached in other works of his.

Gersonides was more restrained in his appreciation of Ibn Rushd than those Jewish Averroists who displayed an exaggerated admiration for their model, seeing him as the one 'who reconciled true religion with truth itself', and even went so far as to call the *Tahafut* 'the book of the Alliance' (Moses Narboni).[8] As a mathematician whose works were recognised outside his own community (Pope Clement VI had some of his works translated into Latin), on this point Gersonides had little respect for Ibn Rushd, who rejected the idea of infinite lines in geometry and excluded mathematical concepts from the agent Intellect. He points out certain childish aspects in Ibn Rushd's philosophical argumentation and recognises that his admiration for Aristotle sometimes led him to distort the truth.

AN AMBIGUOUS AUDIENCE

Ibn Rushd nevertheless remains almost his only contact with ancient philosophy. It is through him that he finds the solution he wants when he rejects that of Ibn Rushd himself – for example, on the theory of the intellect, where Gersonides rejects both Themistius and Ibn Rushd in favour of Alexander of Aphrodisias.

Gersonides was strongly contested by the Jewish Averroists, but ultimately recognised by many. Together with Maimonides, he became the target of Hasday Crescas in the fifteenth century. This was the time when Ghazali's *Tahafut al-Falasifa* appeared in Hebrew (1411), although Ibn Rushd's reply to this work had been known in Hebrew since 1328. However, this was not enough to put an end to Ibn Rushd's authority, and he retained some fierce defenders up until the Renaissance, in other words as long as Jewish philosophy continued to flourish. His influence even made itself felt on non-philosophical thinkers. In the *Well of Exile* by Maharal of Prague, who rejects Ibn Rushd and the other Scholastics as obsolete, the conclusion nevertheless includes a quotation from Ibn Rushd to show the agreement between the Torah and philosophy.

THE MEDIEVAL CHRISTIAN ORIENTALISTS

The translations of philosophy made in Toledo and the Ebro valley in the twelfth and thirteenth centuries introduced to the West some of the works of Aristotle and a few independent Arab writers (Qusta b. Luqa, al-Kindi). However, the works transmitted by preference were the Platonic Arabic texts from the *Liber de causis* (from Proclus) to Ibn Sina. It was not until the middle of the thirteenth century that Ibn Rushd's work began to have any impact. There were doubtless numerous channels of transmission, the main ones being Jewish emigrés from Spain, and Michael Scott who, having worked in Toledo with the help of Andrew the Jew, worked in Palermo for Frederick II as an astrologer and translator of texts on physics and astrology until his death in 1235.

E. Gilson describes the rise in Ibn Rushd's influence: its beginning is fixed by a text of Roger Bacon at shortly after 1230, with decisive stages marked by Albertus Magnus' extensive use of Ibn Rushd around 1250, by Thomas Aquinas who explicitly quotes Averroes no less than five hundred and three times,[9] and finally by the work of Siger de Brabant who impresses it with a particular character. This work is not the place to study the vast movement that has been called 'Latin Averroism' and on which, without denying its importance, certain critics have been able to cast doubt concerning the legitimacy of its name, at its beginning at last, preferring to see it as 'a specifically Parisian paganism' (F. van Steenberghen). This complex movement was cut off from its origins since the medieval authors knew nothing of the lives of those they studied, relegating both Aristotle and Averroes to the same corner of 'Antiquity'. It is interesting, in contrast, to see the attitude of those few authors who did know Arabic and were in a position to understand the precise context.

The two most important 'orientalists' are the Catalans Ramon Marti (c.1230–c.1285) and Ramon Lull (1232–1316). However, each of them adopts a completely different approach, a fact which is highly indicative of the ambiguity of Ibn Rushd's audience.

Ramon Marti was a Dominican, strongly cast in the 'intellectual' mould. He was an expert not only in Arabic but also in Hebrew and Aramaic, and aspects of his knowledge of Arabic thought may have come from his contact with the Jewish intellectual world. He had been a follower of Albertus Magnus in Paris and, as such, must have come into contact with Thomas Aquinas. His major work, *Pugio Fidei*, has many points in common with the *Summa contra gentiles*. If the former is dated 1278 while the latter goes back to 1264, it is quite possible that the Arabic texts used in the *Summa contra gentiles*, particularly the *Tahafut al-tahafut* which was not yet translated, were transmitted by Marti.[10]

The *Pugio* quotes a large number of Arab writers, but in particular Ibn Sina, Ghazali and Ibn Rushd. The works of Ibn Rushd that are used are the brief commentary on the *Metaphysics*, the large commentary on the *Topics*, the commentary on Ibn Sina's medical poem, the *Fasl al-maqal* and its appendix, the brief *Damima* (on divine knowledge of singulars) of which he gives a complete Latin translation under the title of *Epistola ad amicum*, and finally the *Tahafut*.[11]

His documentation is carried out with care. The references are precise, which is unusual for the period. Not just the title but long extracts of the works are almost always quoted. An Arabic scholar, M. Kassem, has also praised the precision of the translation of the *Damima*.

Unlike Marti, Ramon Lull was an 'amateur' and had no professional connections. His contacts with the Arab world were partly of an intellectual nature (he dealt with the logic of Ghazali's *Maqasid al-Falasifa* and Ibn Sab'in's *Budd al-'arif*), but primarily

AN AMBIGUOUS AUDIENCE

they were personal – physical even. Whilst Lull granted considerable importance to 'Averroes' during the periods he spent in Paris, 'Ibn Rushd' did not figure at all in his work destined for a Muslim audience. Furthermore, he felt no need to complete his work in the first of these settings by taking advantage of his knowledge of Arabic.[12]

Renan's statement that Lull saw Averroism as 'Islamism in philosophical form' (p.255) has been frequently reiterated. Some recently published texts have enabled us to correct this judgement.[1] The texts vary widely in tone: pure polemic (*Disputatio Raimundi*; *Sermones contra errores Averrois*), chains of syllogisms, application of the *Ars generalis* which is the creation of the author himself, and finally mystical outbursts (*Liber natalis pueri Iesu*) succeeding and mixing with one another (*L. lamentationis philosophiae*). Lull constantly shifts from one literary genre to another completely opposite one (*disputatio*, liturgical and allegorical drama) so as to build up an entire mental universe right down to its finest details: the theory of Divine Dignities, theory of correlatives, subordination of philosophy to theology . . . not forgetting the symbolic meanings of numbers.

The *Liber natalis* is most forceful in its polemic, since it attacks Averroes directly and not just the Averroists, demanding of the King of France 'quod . . . libros et dicta Averrois expelleret et extrahi faceret de Parisiensi studio, taliter quod nullus de cetero auderet allegare, legere vel audire. . . .' (p.69; cf. also *De divina unitate*, p.212; *Contra errores Averrois*, p.246). This demand is accompanied by a call for the creation of colleges of oriental languages to train missionaries, the unification of the military orders and the allocation of a budget for the Crusades. However, it is only after the philosophical problems have been dealt with that Lull refers explicitly to the 'Sarracenus populus' stating that they will be unable to withstand the alliance of all these forces.

Thus his spirit incorporates both unity in the struggle on the two fronts, and distinction between the two levels:

(1) Just as, as a missionary, he aims for the union of all humanity within a single Christianity, so as a philosopher he foreshadows the struggle against the subsequent developments of political Averroism (the *Defensor pacis* of Marcilus of Padua dates from 1324) confining Pontifical Power to moral authority alone. According to Lull, world unity can be assured only through respect for the natural hierarchy expounded by the allegorical figure of

Justitia: 'Quidquid est in mundo, totum est meum, quia Deus et ego idem sumus. Et ideo bene constitui unum vicarium absolutum, cardinales, principes, praelatos, ut justitiam teneant, et in terra sit pax et tranquillitas; et hoc facientes evadent periculum animarum' (p.65).

(2) While the theory of the double truth is ascribed to the Averroists (certainly hardening their true position), Lull looks for the source of this error in the negation of the role as universal principles of the *Dignitates Divinae*, which was precisely the doing of Averroes. Strangely, the great enemy Islam is not mentioned in the consideration of philosophy. The Truth challenges 'Judaei, falsi philosophi et quicumque alii qui contra istam veritatem veniunt' (p.59). If the 'false philosopher' Averroes and the 'Averroists' are linked in Lull's mind to the Jews, it is most probably because he knows nothing of the work of the Muslim thinker himself. He was only familiar with the catalogue of mistakes concerning Averroes and Aristotle composed by an unknown author, and himself refers exclusively to the condemnations of Etienne Tempier. He only knew (fairly poorly) the works of the Parisian masters, and (by hearsay, through his contacts with the rabbis of Barcelona) that of the Jewish Averroists which gave rise to the great debate over the study of philosophy and the sciences that took place some years prior to the texts considered here. Lull was certainly not one to shy away from unjustified conjectures: in the *L. de acquisitione Terrae Sanctae* written in Montpellier in 1309, he reproached the Muslims for having only rudimentary ideas on the Divine Attributes ('parum sciunt').

A passage in the *Lamentatio Philosophiae* (p.104) helps clarify Lull's view. When he talks about the *Sarraceni*, it is their 'belief' that interests him (cf. also *De syllogismis*, p.197), and when he discusses *Averroista*, it is his manner of 'intelligere' that is in question.

In the *L. natalis* too, nothing suggests that Lull sees Averroes as a specifically Muslim thinker. He is simply the authority invoked by his European (Christian and Jewish) opponents to a vision of the world based on the dynamism of the divine attributes – a vision which *at the same time* Lull had extreme difficulty in making his Muslim interlocutors accept. This is borne out by the *Lamentatio Raimuni* with which he ends the work, and in which he complains both of having suffered in vain in the world of Islam and of having seen his *Art* scorned in Paris (p.72). Even more, the *Sermones contra errores Averrois* composed just three months later draws a clear

AN AMBIGUOUS AUDIENCE

and immediate opposition between Averroes and the Muslims: 'Saraceni autem licet sint infideles, Averroim, qui etiam erat Saracenus, lapidaverunt propter errores, quos contra legem eorum indicebat, nec rationes ipsius non est aliquis eorum ausus palam divulgare' (p.246). There may be a coincidence between the theses upheld by the two sides – hence Averroes denies the Incarnation as do all Muslims, but also does so as a result of his philosophy 'per sensum et imaginationem' (p.257) – but Lull establishes no link between the two.

Thus on the one hand, Ramon Marti makes use of Ibn Rushd in a scrupulous but impersonal way (the argumentation of the *Pugio* is borrowed from Saint Thomas and from current aspects of the polemic between religions). Ramon Lull, on the other hand, is guilty of grave factual errors – even dishonesty – but sets out a completely new path which was to have considerable repercussions, although it was marginalized by the 'philosophically non-professional' character which permeates it. This paradox is doubtless a result of the paradox presented by Ibn Rushd himself. He left behind a written work, but one which was destined to take on a new existence. R. Marti makes use of certain theological texts (it is, however, typical that he does not use the *Kashf*), but taken out of context they could not but be absorbed by the 'commentary aspect' of Ibn Rushd's work. It is true that Marti did carry on personal discussions with the Muslims with all the particular psychological effects this must have entailed, but this does not seem to have had any connection with his philosophical work. Lull is more of a strategist and keeps these two aspects together. In his time, Ibn Rushd was no longer any more than a 'name' in the Muslim milieu, and he sensed intuitively that it would be pointless, either in the Islamic world or in the face of Parisian Averroism, to revive this name. This provides further indirect proof of the discrepancy between the true thought of the sixth/ twelfth-century Cordoban writer and the way in which it could be exploited in radically different contexts.

NOTES

INTRODUCTION

1 See my study: 'La Pensée religieuse des Mozarabes face à l'Islam' (*Traditio* XXXIX, 1983, pp.419–32).

2 See S.M. Stern: 'Ibn Masarra, Follower of Pseudo-Empedocles – An Illusion' (*Actas do IV Congresso de Estudos Arabes e Islamicos*, Leyden, 1971, pp.325–37). See also my study: 'Sur les débuts de la pensée spéculative en Andalus' (*Mélanges de l'Université Saint-Joseph* L, 1984, pp.707–17).

3 H. Mones edition, *Revista del Instituto Egipcio de Estudios Islamicos en Madrid* III, 1955, pp.110–13.

4 Incomplete manuscript in the Escorial: Derembourg and Levi-Provençal, no.1483.

5 Reconstructive essay in J.F.P. Hopkins: 'The Almohad Hierarchy' (*B.S.O.A.S.*, 1954, pp.93–112).

1 THE MAJOR OPTIONS

1 B.R. Goldstein, *Al-Bitrûji: On the Principles of Astronomy. An Edition of the Arabic and Hebrew Versions with Translation* . . . (2 vols, New Haven and London, 1971).

2 Translated by S. Pines, 'La Dynamique d'Ibn Bâjja' (*L'Aventure de la science. Mélanges Alexandre Koyré*, vol. I, 1964, pp.442–68), p.444.

3 R. Arnaldez, 'L'Histoire de la pensée grecque vue par les Arabes' (*Bull. Soc. Fr. Philo.* 72, 3, 1978, p.168).

4 Edited and translated by A. Gonzalez-Palencia (Madrid, 1914).

5 A.J. Elamrani-Jamal, 'Les Rapports de la logique et de la grammaire d'après le Kitâb al-Masâ'il d'al-Batalyawsî (444–522 = 1052–1127)' (*Arabica* XXVI, I, 1979, pp.76–89), pp.80–5.

6 Ibid., pp.80–6.

3 A 'HUMAN' KNOWLEDGE

1 Ibn Mada': *Kitab al-radd 'ala-l-nuha* (ed. Shawqi Dayf, Cairo, 1947).

2 *Aristotelis opera cum Averrois commentariis*, vol.V, F.85 r. Revised by N. Rescher: *Studies in Arabic Philosophy*, Ch.VII: 'Temporal Modalities in Arabic Logic' (Pittsburgh, 1966, p.102).

NOTES TO PAGES 98–129

3 *Ma ba'd al-tabi'a* (ed. M. al-Qabbani, Cairo, undated (possibly 1907), pp.40–1).

4 AN AMBIGUOUS AUDIENCE

1 Cf. my studies: 'La Vie intellectuelle et spirituelle dans les Baléares musulmanes' (*Al-Andalus* XXXVII, 1, 1972, pp.87–132; in particular pp.116–19), and *Penser l'Islam. Les Présupposes islamiques de l' 'Art' de Lull* (Paris, 1980, pp.41–62).

2 Cf. M. Asin: *Introduccion al arte de la logica por Abentomlus de Alcira* (Madrid, 1916).

3 Ibn Sab'in: *Budd al-'arif* (ed. J. Kattura, Beirut, 1978, p.143).

4 Translation H. Corbin, *L'Imagination créatrice dans le soufisme d'Ibn 'Arabi* (Paris, 1958, pp.34–5).

5 Cf. G. Vajda: *Isaac Albalag, averroiste juif, traducteur et annotateur d'al-Ghazali* (Paris, 1960).

6 Quoted by C. Touati: *La Pensée philosophique et théologique de Gersonide* (Paris, 1973, p.31).

7 Ibid., pp.31–2.

8 Quoted by C. Tonati, ibid., p.91.

9 Cf. C. Vansteenkiste O.P.: 'San Tommaso d'Aquino ed Averroè' (*Rivista degli Studi Orientali* XXXII, 1957, pp.585–623).

10 Cf. J.M. Casciaro: *El dialogo teologico de Santo Tomas con Musulmanes y Judios* (Madrid, 1969, pp.44–6).

11 Cf. A. Cortabarria: 'Los textos arabes de Averroes en el "Pugio Fidei" del Dominico R. Marti' (*Actas del congreso internacional de Malaga*, 1986, pp.185–204).

12 Cf. R. Imbach: 'Lulle face aux Averroïstes parisiens' (*Raymond Lulle et le Pays d'Oc*; Cahiers de Fanjeaux 22, 1987, pp.261–82).

13 *Raimundi Lulli Opera Latina*, vol. VII, *Parisiis anno MCCCXI composita* (ed. H. Harada, Turnhout, 1975). This collection does not contain every one of Lull's anti-averroist texts. See also H. Riedlinger: 'Ramon Lull und Averroes nach dem *Liber reprobationis aliquorum errorum Averrois*' (*Scientia Augustiniana*, Festschrift Adolar Zumkeller, Wurzburg, 1975, pp.184–99).

BIBLIOGRAPHICAL GUIDE

HISTORY OF RUSHDIAN STUDIES

Few authors have generated such a controversial image as Ibn Rushd. It is therefore essential to have some idea of this development in order to embark upon a study of the man and his work.

Until the nineteenth century the dominant image given in the Histories of Philosophy, shaped by Latin Averroism, was that of the archetypal godless philosopher. See, for example, the most famous of these works:

Brucker, J.J., *Historia critica Philosophiae* (Lipsiae, 1742–67) III: 97–101. It should nevertheless be noted that this analyst considers Ibn Rushd's interpretation as that corresponding most closely to true Aristotelian thought, which itself had a naturalist and immanentist character.

It is true that 'Averroes' is viewed merely as a commentator and, from the seventeenth century, he was frequently blamed for having replaced the study of nature with that of the 'Master's' work. However, there are certain exceptions: The German scholar B. Keckerman (1571–1609), who was a pioneer in the development of an awareness of the historical conditioning of problematics, and who wanted to disseminate systematic presentation of doctrines, hoped for the emergence of a translator who could save Averroes' works from the state of crudity in which they had been left by the preceding interpreters: 'Then we could see the great services that this Arab rendered to philosophy' (*In praecognitis logicis*, tract. II, cap. II, num. 32).

The famous P. Bayle quotes these words, but in order to refute them. He repeats various bizarre anecdotes quoted by Leo the

BIBLIOGRAPHICAL GUIDE

African, and the usual criticisms of the thesis of the unity of the understanding and accusations of impiety. However, he adds, 'It is amazing that such sublime geniuses as Aristotle and Averroes should have forged so many myths concerning the understanding; but I also dare to say that they would not have formulated them had they not been great geniuses; it was through their acute powers of penetration that they discovered problems that obliged them to leave the beaten track and reject a number of other paths in which they could not find what they were seeking' ('Averroes', *Dictionnaire historique et critique*: remark E).

Around the same period a certain Dupont-Bertris (*Eloges et caractères des philosophes les plus célèbres*, Paris, 1726) launched an attack on historical prejudices, declaring that 'only a biased spirit and an overactive imagination could suggest that Averroes' works turn the reader to impiety' (p.135). While he believes that Averroes does not appear to have 'sampled any religion (since) he was a philosopher dedicated entirely to the lights of his reason', he nevertheless considers that 'the term scoundrel is totally inappropriate for Averroes' (pp.136–8).

Strangely, it was the great inquisitor Francisco Alvarado – called 'El Filosofo Rancio' (the antiquated philosopher), a title which he accepted in his polemic against the ideas of the Luminaries – who praised Averroes in opposition to the followers of the latter and who acted as a general apologist for the learning transmitted to Europe, and Spain in particular, by the Arabs (*Cartas Filosoficas*, vol. 5, Madrid, 1825, pp.69–73).

In his work *Averroès et l'Averroïsme* E. Renan rejects this stance and explores the line of thought taken by Dupont-Bertris although he certainly knew nothing of it. First written in 1852, the work is presented as an 'historical essay' in which the method of investigation is significant in itself. Ibn Rushd is depicted as promoting a thought without dogmatic motivation. However, as a result of the difficulties of documentation, the work deals less with Averroes than with Averroism. In 1861 a new revised edition appeared taking into account the work of Arabists such as Munk, Müller, etc. In this new form, which was to be further improved until 1882, the work remained an essential starting point despite being superseded on many points. The main works of the Arabists who made this new initiative possible include:

Historical studies, in particular:

IBN RUSHD (AVERROES)

Munk, S.: *Mélanges de Philosophie juive et arabe* (Paris, 1857; new edition 1927 and subsequently), pp.418–58.

Previously unknown Arabic texts of Ibn Rushd (Renan had worked only on Latin and occasionally Hebrew translations). The main stages of this return to the sources are:

In 1859, M.J. Müller made known the three theological texts (*Fasl*, *Kashf* and *Damima*) (Münich). The translations appeared after hi. death in 1875 under the title: *Philosophie und Theologie von Averroes* (Munich). The 1859 edition served as the basis for the Cairo editions of 1313/1895 and subsequent years.

In 1869 J. Hercz published from the Hebrew: *Drei Abhandlungen über die Conjunction des separaten Intellektes mit dem Menschen* (Berlin).

F. Lasinio then published in succession: *Il commento medio di Averroe alla Poetica di Aristotele* (Arabic and Hebrew; *Annali delle Universita Toscane*, Pisa, 1872) and *Il commento medio di Averroe alla Retorica di Aristotele* (Florence, 1877).

'Branno fin qui sconosciuto del Commento Medio (Talkhis) alla Topica di Aristotele' (*ASISO* 1, 1873, pp.125–59, and 2, 1874, pp.234–67).

Freudenthal, J. and Fränkel, S.: *Die durch Averroes erhaltene Fragmente Alexanders zur Metaphysik des Aristoteles* (*Abhandl. d. kgl. Akad. d. Wis Zu Berlin*, 1884).

Tahafut al-Tahafut (Cairo, 1302/1884 and subsequent years).

Ma ba'd al-Tabi'a (brief commentary on the *Metaphysics*), ed. M. al-Qabbani (Cairo, 1303/1885 and subsequent years).

Hannes, L.: *Des Averroes Abhandlungen 'Ueber die Möglichkeit des Conjunktion' oder 'Ueber den materialen Intellekt'* (Halle, 1892), from the Hebrew.

Horten, M.: *Die Metaphysik des Averroes* (*Anhandlungen zur Philosophie und ihrer Geschichte* **XXXVI**, 1912).

Morata, N.: *Los opusculos de Averroes en la Biblioteca del Escorial. I. El opusculo de la union del entendimiento agente con el hombre* (El Escorial, 1923).

Bergh, S. van den: *Die Epitome der Metaphysik des Averroes* (Leiden, 1924).

Bouyges, M.: ed. of the *Talkhis Kitab al-Maqulat* (Beirut, 1932)

BIBLIOGRAPHICAL GUIDE

and of the *Tafsir ma ba'd al-Tabi'a* (large commentary on the *Metaphysics*) (3 vols, Beirut, 1938–48).

Rosenthal, F.: 'Averroes' paraphrase on Plato's *Politeia*' (*J.R.A.S.*, 1934, pp.736–44) and *Averroes' Commentary on Plato's Republic* (Cambridge, 1956), from the Hebrew.

This progressive exploration explains the uneven character of the studies made on Ibn Rushd, since many writers were content simply to pursue old themes or, at best, the analyses (and prejudices) of Renan. It has nevertheless served as a basis for various corrective works, amongst which those worthy of note are:

Bouyges, M.: 'Inventaire des textes arabes d'Averroès' (*Mélanges de l'Université Saint Joseph* VIII, Beirut, 1922, pp.1–54; IX, 1924, pp.43–8).

Wolfson, H.A.: 'Plan of a Corpus Commentariorum Averrois in Aristotelem' (*Speculum* VI, 1931, pp.412–27, and *Studies in the History of Philosophy and Religion* I, Cambridge, Mass., 1973, pp.430–54).

The most prominent aspect of Rushdian research is the polemic concerning Ibn Rushd's religious stance. A good summary of this, mentioning the works of Renan, Mehren (1888), Asin Palacios (1904), Gauthier (1909 to 1948), Horten (1913), Bonucci and Nallino (1916) and Alonso (1947) can be found in Badawi, A.: *Histoire de la Philosophie en Islam* vol. II: *Les Philosophes purs* (Paris, 1972), pp.766–76.

See also Rosemann, Ph.W.: 'Averroes. A catalogue of editions and scholarly writings from 1821 onwards' (*Bulletin de Philosophie Médiévale*, vol. 30, 1988, pp.153–221).

Once the reader has been alerted to the methodological caution that this history suggests for dealing with the various editions and studies, a reading of Ibn Rushd can be resumed based on documents which, though not yet published in their entirety, nevertheless still appear fairly representative.

HISTORICAL SOURCES

Ibn al-Abbar: *Al-Takmila li-Kitab al-Sila* (Renan, pp.435–7. Ed. Codera, *Biblioteca Arabico-Hispana* V–VI, Madrid, 1887–9, biogr. no. 853. Ed. 'I.'A. Husayni, 2 vols, Cairo and Baghdad, 1955–6;

IBN RUSHD (AVERROES)

vol. II, in particular pp.542, 554 and 941). This author is fundamental because he emphasizes Ibn Rushd's position within the traditional Andalusian framework.

Abu 'Abd Allah al-Ansari: *Kitab al-Dhayl wa-l-Takmila* (fragments in Renan, pp.437–47. Beirut edition currently in progress). On this work see al-Ahwani, 'A.'A.: *Revista del Institut. Egip. de Estud. Islam. en Madrid* (1953, pp.1–16, Arabic). Continues in the Andalusian tradition with numerous anecdotes requiring a highly critical reading.

Abd a. Wahid al-Marrakushi: *Al-Mu'jib fi-talkhis akhbar al Maghrib* (Renan, trans. pp.16–17. Ed. Dozy: *The History of the Almohades*, 2nd edn, Leiden, 1881, pp.174–5 and 222. French translation, Fagnan: *Histoire des Almohades*, Algiers, 1893, pp.209–10. New edition by M.S. 'Aryan, Cairo, 1963). Contains the famous accounts of the meetings with the Almohad rulers.

Ibn Abi Usaybi'a: *'Uyun al-inba' fi-tabaqat al-atibba'* (Renan, pp.448–56. Ed. A. Müller, vol. II, Cairo, 1882, pp.75–8. New edition N. Rida, Beirut, 1965). Gives the viewpoint of the historian of sciences.

Al-Dhahabi: *Tarikh al-Islam* (Renan, pp.456–62) and Ibn Farhun: *Al-Dibaj al-Mudhahhab* (2nd edn, Cairo, 1943, p.284), are primarily compilers of the works cited above. The later historians contribute nothing further except, especially in the case of Leo the African, fantastic anecdotes.

See also:

Morata, N.: 'La Présentation de Averroes en la corte almohade' (*La Ciudad de Dios*, CLIII, 1941, pp.101–22).

Alonso, M.: *Teologia de Averroes (Estudio y documentos)* (Madrid-Granada, 1947), especially pp.43–98.

Cruz Hernandez, M.: *Historia de la Filosofia Hispano-musulmana* (II, Madrid, 1957, pp.7–205), and numerous later works synthesized in Abn l-Walid, *Ibn Rushd (Averroes). Vida, obra, pensamiento, influencia (Cordoba, 1986).*

To locate Ibn Rushd with respect to the contemporary intellectual environment and major cultural trends, see:

Urvoy, D.: *Le Monde des ulemas andalous du V/XIe au VII/XIII siècle* (Geneva, 1978), especially pp.178–81.

BIBLIOGRAPHICAL GUIDE

TEXTS

Occidental Arab writers

This includes writers providing an immediate context for Ibn Rushd's work (which obviously also includes Arabic translations of ancient texts (particularly Aristotle and his commentators, but also certain texts of Plato, Galen and even traditions descended from Stoicism) and oriental *Falsafa* (Farabi and Ibn Sina), which would require too much space to give here).

Ibn Bajja (d. 533/1139)

Ibn Bajja, M. Asin Palacios, 'Avempace botanico' (*Al-Andalus* V, 1940, pp.255–65).

— M. Asin Palacios, 'Tratado de Avempace sobre la union del intelecto con el hombre' (*Al-Andalus* VII, 1942, pp.1–42).

— *El regimen del solitario* (ed. and trans. M. Asin Palacios, Madrid-Granada, 1946).

— *Kitab al-Nafs* (ed. al-Ma'sumi, Damascus, 1965).

— *Rasa'il Ibn Bajja al-ilahiya* (ed. M. Fakhry, Beirut, 1968).

Ibn Tumart (d. 524/1130)

Ibn Tumart, *Le Livre de Mohammed Ibn Toumert, Mahdi des Almohades* (ed. D. Luciani, Algiers, 1903, pp.229–44).

— E. Lévi-Provençal, 'Six fragments inédits d'une chronique anonyme du début des Almohades' (*Mélanges René Basset*, Paris, 1925, vol. II, pp.355–6 and 385–6; the 'prayer' of the Mahdi).

— E. Lévi-Provençal, *Documents inédits d'histoire almohade* (Paris, 1928; text pp.1–10, trans. pp.1–15; the 'Letters to the community').

— M.T. d'Alverny and G. Vajda, 'Marc de Tolède traducteur d' Ibn Tumart' (*Al-Andalus*, 1951, pp.282–3; Latin translation of a *murshida*).

— H. Massé, 'La Profession de foi et les guides spirituels du Mahdi Ibn Toumert' (*Mémorial Henri Basset*, vol. II, Paris, 1928, pp.105–21).

See also:

Talbi, M.: 'Ibn Tumart' (*Les Africains*, ed. C.A. Julien *et al.*, vol. 11, Paris, 1978, pp.135–65).

Urvoy, D.: 'La Pensée d'Ibn Tûmart' (*Bulletin d'Etudes Orientales* XXVII, 1974, pp.19–44).

Ibn Tufayl (d. 581/1185–6)

Ibn Turayl, *Hayy ibn Yaqzan* (numerous editions of the Arabic text, notably L. Gauthier, cf. below).

— E. Pocock, *Philosophus autodidactus sive Epistola Abi Jaafar ibn Thofail de Hai ebn Yoqdhan in qua ostenditur quomodo ex Inferiorum contemplatione ad Superiorum Notitiam Ratio humana ascendere possit, ex arabica in linguam latinam versa* (Oxonii, 1671).

— *The improvement of human reason. Exhibited in the life of Hai Ebn Yokdhan. Written in Arabic above 500 years ago by Abu Jaafar Ebn Tophail. In which is demonstrated by what methods one may, by the meer light of nature, attain the knowledge of things natural and supernatural; more particularly the knowledge of God . . . New translated from the original Arabic by S. Ockley* (1708; re-ed. 1983).

— Ibn Thofail: *Hayy Ben Yaqdhan. Roman philosophique* (ed. and French trans. by L. Gauthier, Paris, 3rd edn, 1984).

— E. Garcia Gomez, 'Una qasida politica inedita de Ibn Tufayl' (*Rev. Inst. Eg. Est. Isl.* I, 1953, pp.21–8/29–32).

Ibn Rushd

Since a number of texts are still unknown in the original, the edition generally used is the Venetian Latin edition (reprod. photo.).

Opera omnia Aristotelis Stagiritae . . . cum Averrois Cordubensis in ea opera Commentariis (Venetiis, MDLX; apud Cominum de Tridino (11 vols). See the index of Rushdian texts from this edition in Alonso, M.: *Teologia de Averroes* (Madrid-Granada, 1947), pp.5–10.

The most complete and convenient bibliography (listing known manuscripts as well as Arabic, Hebrew and Latin texts of each work validated by one of them) is that of:

BIBLIOGRAPHICAL GUIDE

Gomez Nogales, S.: 'Bibliografia sobre las obras de Averroes' (*Multiple Averroès. Actes du colloque international organisé à l'occasion du 850e anniversaire de la naissance d'Averroès. Paris 20–23 septembre 1976* (Paris, 1978, pp.351–87), supplemented by a list of 'Oeuvres d'Averroès en traduction hébraïsques imprimées' (p.389). Mention is also made of texts that have been completely lost but that are given in ancient lists in Badawi, 'A.: *Histoire de la Philosophie en Islam* (Paris, 1972, pp.745–59).

The te.ts used in this study and those currently most easily accessible are the following:

Theological texts

Hourani, G.F.: *Ibn Rushd (Averroes) Kitab Fasl al-Maqal . . .* (Arabic text; Leiden, 1959).
— *Averroes' On the harmony of religion and philosophy*, a transl. with introd. and notes of *K. Fasl al-Maqal* (*Gibb Mem. Series N.S.* XXI, London, 1961).
For a recent edition of the *Fasl*, that of M. 'Amara (Beirut, 1981) may be used.
Manahij al-adilla fi 'aqa'id al-Milla (ed. M. Qasim, Cairo, 1969). English translation of extracts in Hourani (see above) and of the greater part of the work in Sweetman, J.W.: *Islam and Christian Theology* (London, 1965, part II, vol. II, pp.82–189).
Complete Spanish translation by Alonso, M.: *Teologia de Averroes* (Madrid-Granada, 1947, pp.203–355).
Tahafut al-Tahafut: the quotations have been taken from the Bouyges edition (Beirut, 1930). The van den Bergh translation (see below) is based on this. *Averroes' 'Tahafut al-Tahafut (The Incoherence of the Incoherence)*, trans. with Introduction and Notes by Simon van den Bergh (2 vols, London, 1969). Also available is the more recent edition by S. Dunya (2 vols, Cairo, 1965). An essential work because of its quality and accurate notes. An important introduction to the author's more personal work.

Juridical texts

Bidayat al-Mujtahid wa nihayat al-Muqtasid: numerous Arabic editions, in particular: 2 vols, Cairo, 1353/1935; ed. 'A. Mahmud and 'A.H. Mahmud, Cairo, undated; etc.

IBN RUSHD (AVERROES)

— Partial translation by A. Laïmeche (3 vols, Algiers, 1926–40). A useful translation, but too inaccurate.

— New translation of the Introduction by L. Bercher (*Revue Tunisienne de Droit*, 1955, pp.31–7).

Medical texts

Kitab al-Kulliyat fi-l-Tibb (photographic edition of the Arabic text of the Sacro Monte manuscript; Larache, 1939).

— (ed. J.M. Forneas Besteiro, Madrid-Granada, 1987).

Colliget: Latin trans. by Bonacosa (1255) (ed. Venice, 1482, 1553). The introduction and Books I and II are reproduced in facsimile in the work of E. Torre (cf. below).

Commentaria Averrois in Galenum (trans. M.C. Vazquez de Benito, Madrid, 1984).

Anawati, G.C. and Zayed, S.: *Rasâ'il Ibn Rushd al-tibbiyya* (Cairo, 1987). Translation: Anawati, G.C. and Ghalioungui, P.: *Medical Manuscripts of Averroes at El Escorial* (Cairo, 1986).

Commentaries on Aristotle

Since 1978 the 'International Academic Union' (Thomas Institute of Cologne) has taken up the work of editing the commentaries:

Hoffman, R.: 'Corpus Commentariorum Averrois in Aristotelem: Protokoll der Tagung über das Corpus Averroicum vom 16. bis 17–3–1978 in Koln' (*Bull. Philo. Med.* 20, 1978, pp.58–64).

Extensive work editing Arabic, Hebrew and Latin texts is currently in progress, giving access to hitherto neglected texts. However, this is evidently a long-term project and co-ordination is not easy (cf. the remarks of H. Daiber in *Der Islam* 62, 1, 1985, p.146). Besides the works used in this study, also given here are those works which complete S. Gomaz Nogales' bibliography mentioned above (for the somewhat outdated main editions, see above para. 1).

Averroes' Three Short Commentaries on Aristotle's Topics, Rhetoric and Poetics (ed. and trans. C. E. Butterworth, Albany, 1977).

The middle commentaries on the *Organon* are currently being

BIBLIOGRAPHICAL GUIDE

published under the aegis of the American Research Centre in Egypt: *al-Maqulat* (*Categories*), 1980; *al-I'bara* (*Interpretation*), 1981; *al-Qiyas* (*Prior Analytics*), 1983; *al-Burhan* (*Posterior Analytics*), 1981; *al-Jadal* (*Topics*), 1979 (ed. M. Qasim, supplement by C.E. Butterworth and A. Haridi; Cairo). However, this very careful edition does not replace certain previous editions on all points (cf. Arnaldez, R.: *Der Islam* 62, 1, 1985, pp.141–3). C.E. Butterworth has also undertaken the translation: *Averroes' Middle Commentaries on Aristotle's Categories and De Interpretatione* (Princeton, 1983). The Hebrew text of the middle commentaries on Porphyry's *Isagoge* and the *Categories* and an English translation have been produced by H.A. Davidson (2 vols, Cambridge, Mass., 1962). Finally, almost simultaneously with the Qasim edition, the same editor published the commentary on the *Categories* on the *De Interpretatione* (1976), on the *Topics* (1980) and on the *Sophistical Refutations* (1973), prepared by M.S. Salim, while in Beirut the three volumes of the edition by G. Jehamy were issued: *Averroès, Paraphrase de la Logique d'Aristote* (*Categories, Interprétation, Topiques*; 1982).

Ibn Rushd: Grand Commentaire et Paraphrases des 'Seconds Analytiques' d'Aristote (ed. A. Badawi, Kuwait, 1984). Significant text being with the *tafsir* on *Metaphysics* the only two great commentaries retained in Arabic. See Schöler, G. and Gätjje, H., 'Averroes' Schriften zur Logik. Der araabische Text der 'Zweiten Analytiken' im 'Grossen Kommentor des Averroes' (*Z.D.M.G.*, 1980, 130, 55, pp.557–85).

Talkhis Kitab Aristutalis fi-l-Shi'r (ed. M.S. Salim, Cairo, 1971). Trans. C.E. Butterworth: *Averroes' Middle Commentary on Aristotle's Poetics* (Princeton, 1986).

Talkhis al-Khataba (ed. M.S. Salim, Cairo, 1969).

S. Harvey, 'A 14th-century Kabbalist's excerpts from the last Arabic original of Averroes' Middle Commentary on the Physics' was published in *Studies in Arabic and Islam*, vol. 6 (Jerusalem, 1985, pp.219–27).

Talkhis Kitab al-Sama' (ed. 'Alawi, Fez, 1404/1984).

Averrois Cordubensis Commentarium Medium ★ Epitome in Aristotelis De Generatione et Corruptione Libros. Textum Hebraicum (ed. S. Kurland), Latin trans. (ed. F.H. Forbes and S. Kurland), (Cambridge, Mass., 1958 and 1956, respectively). English trans. of

143

the Middle and Brief Commentary by S. Kurland (Cambridge, Mass., 1958).

Epitome De Anima (trans. S. Gomez Nogales, Madrid, 1985).

Averrois Cordubensis Commentarium Magnum in Aristotelis De Anima Libros (Latin trans., ed. F.S. Crawford, Cambridge, Mass., 1953).

Talkhis Kitab al-Hass wa-'l-mahsus (ed. H. Blumberg, Cambridge, Mass., 1972). *Averrois Cordubensis compendia librorum Aristotelis qui parva Naturalia vocantur. Textum Hebraicum* (ed. H. Blumberg, Cambridge, Mass., 1954), Latin trans. (ed. A.L. Shields and H. Blumberg, Cambridge, Mass., 1949).

Averroes. Epitome of Parva Naturalia (trans. H. Blumberg, Cambridge, Mass., 1961).

Averroes. Epitome in Physicorum Libros (Arabic text, J. Puig, Madrid, 1983; trans. Madrid, 1987).

The Bouyges edition of the Arabic text of the Large Commentary on the *Metaphysics* (Beirut, 1922) has been the object of criticism, notably from A. Badawi who accuses it of being insufficiently critical. However, it remains the only existing one. There are also two partial translations available:

Ibn Rushd's Metaphysics: A translation with introduction of Ibn Rushd's commentary on Aristotle's Metaphysics, Book Lam by C. Genequand (Leiden, 2nd edn, 1986). It is worth referring to the highly critical review by D. Gutas in *Der Islam* (64, 1, 1987, pp. 122–6) which points out numerous corrections.

Averroes: Grand commentaire de la 'Metaphysique' d'Aristote; livre lam-lambda. Traduit de l'arabe et annoté par Aubert Martin (Paris, 1984). Published by the University of Liège (Belgium).

For the Commentary on Plato's *Republic*, besides the edition of the Hebrew text with trans. by F. Rosenthal (Cambridge, 1956), a new translation by L. Lerner is now available: *Averroes on Plato's Republic* (Ithaca and London, 1974).

Miscellaneous

Averroes' De Substantia Orbis. Critical edn of the Hebrew text with English trans. and comment. by A. Hyman (Cambridge, Mass., 1986).

Ibn Rushd: The epistle on the possibility of conjunction with the active

BIBLIOGRAPHICAL GUIDE

intellect, with the comment of Moses Narboni, ed. and trans. F. Bland (New York, 1982).

'Averroes (Ibn Rushd) on the Modality of Propositions'. Arabic text edited by D.M. Dunlop: *Islamic Studies* I, Karachi, 1962, pp.23–34). Trans. N. Rescher 'Averroes' *Quaesitum* on assertoric (absolute) propositions' (*Studies in the History of Arabic Logic*, Pittsburgh, 1963, pp.91–105).

Maqalat fi-l-Mantiq wa 'ilm al-tabi'i (ed. 'Alawi, Dar al-Bayda', 1983).

CURRENT STATUS OF THE QUESTIONS

This section lists a number of works published recently, according to the degree to which the questions have been developed. This will enable the reader to tackle the particular chapters of the work.

General studies

Arnaldez, R.: 'Ibn Rushd' (*Encyclopédie de l'Islam, nouv. éd.*, vol.III, Leiden, 1971). An essay presenting Ibn Rushd through readings of the major Arabic texts currently known.

Badawi, 'A.: *Histoire de la Philosophie en Islam* (Paris, 1972). A scholarly work, but unevenly developed and somewhat wordy.

Berque, J.: *'Averroès et les contraires', L'ambivalence dans la culture arabe*, ed. J. Berque and J.P. Charnay (Paris, 1967, pp.133–42). A succinct but highly thought-provoking comment.

Cruz Hernandez, M.: cf. *supra*. The most significant attempt to present an 'Averroean system'.

Multiple Averroès (Paris, 1978). A collection of commentaries covering Ibn Rushd's activities in all fields except medicine.

Religious thought

Arnaldez, R.: 'La Pensée religieuse d'Averroès. I. La Doctrine de la création dans le *Tahafut*' (*Studia Islamica* VII, 1957, pp.99–114); II. 'La théorie de Dieu dans le *Tahafut* (*St Islamica* VIII, 1957, pp.15–28); III. 'L'Immortalité de l'âme dans le *Tahafut*' (*St Islamica* X, 1959, pp.23–41). A fundamental work.

Mahdi, M.: 'Remarks on Averroes' *Decisive Treatise*' (*Islamic*

IBN RUSHD (AVERROES)

Theology and Philosophy. Studies in honor of George Hourani, ed. M.E. Marmura, Albany, 1984, pp.188–202).

Juridical works

Brunschvig, R.: 'Averroès juriste' (*Etudes d'Orientalisme dediées à la mémoire de Lévi-Provençal*, vol.1, Paris, 1962, pp.35–68). A pioneering and still unsurpassed work.

Medical works

Bürgel, J.C.: 'Averroes "contra Galenum"' (*Nachrichten d. Akademie d. Wissenschaft in Göttingen* I, 9, 1967, pp.263–70).

Gätje, H.: 'Probleme der *Colliget*-Forschung' (*Zeitschrift d. Deutsche Morgenländische Gesellschaft* 130, 1980, pp.278–303). An examination of textual and doctrinal questions.

Gätje, H.: 'Zur Lehre von den Temperamenten bei Averroes' (*Z.D.M.G.* 132, 1982, pp.243–68).

Rodriguez Molero, F.X.: 'Originalidad y estudio de la anatomia de Averroes' (*Al-Andalus* XV, 1950, pp.47–67). An interesting essay despite its age, since it gives the scientist's point of view.

Torre, E.: *Averroes y la ciencia medica. La doctrina anatomofunctional del 'Colliget'* (Madrid, 1974). Includes the Latin translation of the Introduction and Books I and II based on the Bonacosa version.

Physics and Cosmology

Carmody, E.J.: 'The planetary theory of Ibn Rushd' (*Osiris* 10, 1952, pp.556–86).

Goddu, A.: 'Avicenna, Avempace and Averroes – Arabic sources of "mutual attraction" and their influence on Mediaeval and Modern Conceptions of Attraction and Gravitation' (*Orientalische Kultur und Europäisches Mittelalter*, ed. A. Zimmermann and I. Craemer-Ruegenberg, Berlin–New York, 1985, pp.218–39).

Hugonard-Roche, H.: 'Remarques sur l'évolution doctrinale d'Averroès dans les commentaires au De Caelo: le problème du mouvement de la terre' (*Mélanges de la Casa de Velazquez* XIII, 1977, pp.103–17). Highlights Ibn Rushd's tendencies towards systematization. Includes unedited extracts of the Brief Commentary on *De caelo*.

BIBLIOGRAPHICAL GUIDE

Hugonard-Roche, H.: 'L'Epitomé du De Caelo d'Aristote par Averroès. Questions de méthode et de doctrine' (*Archives d'Histoire Doctrinale et Litteraire du Moyen-Age*, 1984, pp.7–39). Completes the preceding study's development of points of doctrine.

Hugonard-Roche, H.: 'Méthode d'argumentation et philosophie naturelle chez Averroès' (*Orientalische Kultur und Europäisches Mittelalter*, Berlin–New York, pp.240–53).

Palacz, R.: 'Kopernikus und Averroes' (*Studia Mediewistyczne* 22, 1, Warsawa, ed. A. Zimmermann and I. Craemer-Ruegenberg, 1983, pp.105–10).

Sarnowsky, J.: 'Averroes als "scholastischer" Kommentator der Physik des Aristoteles' (*Orientalischer Kultur und Europaisches Mittelalter*, ed. A. Zimmermann and I. Craemer-Ruegenberg, Berlin–New York, 1985, pp.254–73).

Schmieja, H.: 'Drei Prologue im Grossen Physikkommentar des Averroes?' (*Aristotelisches Erbe im arabisch-lateinischen Mittelalter. Übersetzungen, Kommentare, Interpretationen*, ed. A. Zimmermann, Berlin–New York, 1986, pp.175–89).

Metaphysics and theory of the intellect

Davidson, H.A.: 'Averroes on the material intellect' (*Viator*, Los Angeles, 1986, pp.91–137).

Geyer, G.E.: 'Some notes on Averroes and the great commentary on the metaphysics of Aristotle' (*Listening* 9, 1974, pp.38–53).

Hoffmann, R.: 'Ubersetzungbedingte Verständnisprobleme im grossen Metaphysikkommentar des Averroes' (*Aristotelisches Erbe im arabisch-lateinischen Mittelalter. Übersetzungen, Kommentare, Interpretationen*, ed. A. Zimmerman, Berlin–New York, 1986, pp.141–60).

Hyman, A.: 'Averroes as commentator on Aristotle's theory of the intellect' (*Studies in Aristotle*, ed. D.J. O'Meara, Washington, 1981, pp.161–91).

Kogan, B.S.: 'Eternity and origination. Averroes' discourse on the manner of the World's existence' (*Islamic Theology and Philosophy. Studies in honor of George Hourani*, ed. M.E. Marmura, Albany, 1984, pp.203–25).

Kogan, B.S.: *Averroes and the Metaphysics of Causation* (Albany, New

York, 1985). A classical perspective emphasising Ibn Rushd's 'philosophical' stance in the face of Kalam.

Jolivet, J.: Conférences d'Histoire des théologies médiévales, *Annuaire de l'Ecole Pratique des Hautes Etudes. Sciences religieuses.* 1969–70, pp.324–9; 1970–1, pp.317–24; 1971–2, pp.354–7. Studies of key passages which have been widely drawn upon in the current work.

Jolivet, J.: 'Divergences entre les métaphysiques d'Ibn Rushd et d'Aristote' (*Arabica* 29, 1982, pp.225–45). An extremely detailed analysis and very useful summing-up, apart from the often over-emotional defence of Ibn Rushd's originality. Stays within the classical philosophical perspective.

Mohammed, O.N.: *Averroes' doctrine of immortality: A matter of controversy* (Waterloo, Ont., 1984). Useful references.

Moral and political

Berman. L.V.: 'Sophrosyne and enkrateia in Arabic, Latin and Hebrew: The case of the Nichomachean Ethics of Aristotle and its Middle Commentary by Averroes' (*Orientalische Kultur und Europaisches Mittelalter*, ed. A. Zimmermann and I. Craemer-Ruegenberg, Berlin–New York, 1985, pp.274–87).

Butterworth, C.E.: 'Ethics and classical Islamic philosophy. A study of Averroes' commentary on Plato's Republic' (*Ethics in Islam*, ed. R.G. Hovannisian, Malibu, 1985, pp.17–45).

Lazar, L.: 'L'education politique selon Ibn Rushd (Averroës)' (*Studia Islamica* LII, 1980, pp.135–66). A Hebraist's point of view.

Leaman, O.: 'Ibn Rushd on Happiness and Philosophy' (*Studia Islamica* LII, 1980, pp.167–81).

INDEX

Abbasid caliphate 17
Abd al-Mu'min, Sultan 20, 33
Abd al-Rahman al-Labasi 9
Abd Allah b. Jabir 118
Abduh, Muhammed 121
Absolute Being 75
Abu Bakr b. al-Arabi, Grand Qadi of
  Seville (468/1076–543/1148) 9, 15
Abu Bakr Bundud of Cordoba 32
Abu Ja'afar Yusuf b. Hasday 6
Abu Marwan Ibn Zuhr (Avenzoar)
  (c. 484/1091–558/1162) 47
Abu Tamman 60
Abu Ya'qub Yusuf 32, 33, 34
Abu Yusuf Ya'qub (al-Mansur) 34–5,
  118
Abu-l-Ala (d 525/1130) 47, 49
Abu-l-Barakat al-Baghdadi (died
  c. 560/1164) 25, 99
Abu-l-Harith, bishop 6, 122
Abu-l-Qasim Ahmad 29
Abu-l-Salt (b 460/1067) 61
Abu-l-Walid Ibn Rushd al Jadd, *fatawi*
  of 29–30
Abu-l-Walid Muhammad b. Rushd 29,
  30
Abu-l-Walid Muhammad ibn Ahmad
  al-Hafiz 31
Abulcasis *see* al-Zahrawi, Abu-l-Qasim
*Accounts and texts concerning the destruction
  of Ghazali* (al-Ilbiri) 11
adab, tradition of 27–8
addad 97–8
Adoptionism 4
agriculture, 21, 48

al-Andalus 43, 71, 80; logic in 61;
  medicine in 47; philosophical milieu
  6; praised 31; tradition of 28; two
  movements 10
al-Ansari 36, 70
al-Bitruji (Alpetragius) 42, 44–5
al-Farabi (259/872–339/950) 5, 6–7,
  37, 39, 45, 58, 61, 71, 83, 92, 110,
  123, 125; on Aristotle 113; as model
  111–12
al-Ghazali, Abu Hamid
  (450/1059–501/1111) 35, 75,
  78–80, 87, 98, 99, 105, 117, 125,
  127, 128; burning of works 9–10;
  condemnation of 15, 19; on creation
  83; critique of reason 7–9; on
  existence 85; as 'father of
  Almohadism' 26
al-Hakam II 5, 20, 33
al-Idrisi 21
al-Ilbiri, Muhammad
  (458/1064–5–537/1142–3) 11
Al-Islam wa-l-Nasraniya (Abduh) 121
al-Kindi (c. 185/796–260/873) 6, 51,
  59, 127
al-Kulliyat fil-tibb 37, 40, 41, 46, 47,
  48, 54, 115
al-Mahri, Muhammad b. Ibrahim (al-
  Usuli) 35
al-Marrakushi 32
al-Razi, Abu Bakr 25, 51, 52, 82
al-Shafi'i 14
Al-Shatibi 68
al-Sina 39
al-Sirafi 62

INDEX

al-Trujali *see* Ibn Harun de Trujillo
al-Usuli *see* al-Mahri
al-Utbi 30
al-Zahrawi, Abu-l-Qasim (Abulcasis) 51
Alamut 3
Albalag, Isaac 124
Albertus Magnus 6, 25, 52, 127, 128
Alexander of Aphrodisias 43, 96, 127
Ali, Amir (1849–1928) 122
Almohadism 94, 95; crisis of 109; interpretation 81–2
Almohads 1, 8, 57, 64, 76, 113; acceptance of 36; doctrine 12–14, 17, 120; imams 17; legacy of 70; pressure of 10–11; profession of faith 19–21; propaganda 15–16; reforms 11–124; in Spain 29
Almoravids 14, 17, 19; decline of 112; document concerning heretical books 10–11; establishment of 30, 69
Alonso, M. 80, 91
analogy 66–7, 93; juridical 95
anatomy 51–3
Andrew the Jew 127
Andronicus of Rhodes 28, 40
Anselm, Saint 18, 20, 81
Antun, Farah (1874–1922) 120–1
Apocrypha 4
Apollonius of Perga 44
Aquinas, Saint Thomas 87, 124, 127, 128, 131
arguments 114–15; Aristotelian 79
Aristotelian theory 21, 22, 24–5
Aristotle 67, 111, 113, 114; on 'cause' 87; on celestial bodies 42; commentaries 32, 34, 38; and creation 104–5; as guide 40; influence of 123–4; on medicine 49; progress after 59; study of Physics 45–6; thoughts as sovereign truth 55–6; three powers 52; works of 28
Arnaldez, R. 1, 58, 87, 100
Asal 27
Ash'arism 75
Ash'ari 70
Ash'arites 83, 105
Asin Palacios 4
astronomy 39, 41–6

atomist theory 114
Avenzoar *see* Abu Marwan
Averroism 100–1, 124, 127–9, 130–1
Avicenna *see* Ibn Sina
Avicennism 123

Bacon, Roger 127
Badawi, A. 58–9
Bahya b. Paquda 9
Banu Rushd 29, 64
Banu Zuhr 47, 49
Bayan 30
being, necessary and possible 85–6
Berbers 29, 74; social structure 16
Berque, J. 97, 98
Bidayat al-mujtahid wa nihayat al-muqtasid 64–8, 78, 113
Book of Elucidation (Ibn Maymun) 64
Book of Experiments (Ibn Bajja) 48
Braulio of Saragossa 3
Brothers of Purity 5
Brunschvig, R. 64, 78
Budd al-'arif (Ibn Sab'in) 128

Canon of Medicine (Ibn Sina) 48
celestial bodies 42–3, 84–5, 105, 125
Christianity 18
Christians 82; advance of 109; in coalition 35; orientalists 127–31; threat of 70
classicists 60
Classification of the Sciences (al-Farabi) 92
Clement VI, pope 126
Collar of the dove (Ibn Hazm) 28
colour, as example of 'existing things' 87
commentaries 71, 92, 111, 126; brief 37, 39, 43, 55, 61–2; middle 37–8, 39–40, 43, 46, 59, 90, 91, 111; large 38, 44, 45, 62, 77, 101
Commentary on the profession of faith of the imam and Mahdi' (Ibn Tumart) 71
community, human and political 109–15
Compendium (Abu-l-Salt) 61
completeness, principle of 55
Comte, Auguste 1
consensus, as valid 66

150

INDEX

consultations, problem of 15
Corbin, H. 2, 120
Cordoba 29, 35, 71
creation, approach to 104–6; idea of 72;
  question of 82–9
Crescas, Hasday 127
crusades 129
Cruz Hernandez, M. 39, 55

Dalalat al-ha'irin 123
Damima 71
Dayf, Shawqi 94
De Anima 55–6, 91, 101, 102, 103,
  126
De animae beatitudine 38, 108
De caelo et mundo 39, 40, 97, 126
De generatione animalium 40, 55, 126
De generatione et corruptione 126
De partibus animalium 40, 55, 126
De senso et sensato 40
De substantia orbis 38
De vegetabilibus aut plantis (Albertus
  Magnus) 25
Defensor pacis (Marcilus of Padua) 129
Descartes, René 72
diglossia, phenomenon of 122
discourse, 93; assertoric/absolute 95–6;
  hierarchical arrangement 62
divine, action 12; custom 106; wisdom
  106
Divine Dignities, theory of 129

effort, personal 14, 67
elements, four 42, 47, 56
Elipandus, Archbishop of Toledo 4
embryology 52
Encyclopedia of Islam (Arnaldez) 100
enemies 114
enigmas 62
epicycles 42, 44
epigenesis, doctrine of 52
Epitome of logic 39
Escorial 71
eternity 83, 99, 106
eudemony 55
Eudemus 95
Eurocentrist view 2
evolution, problems of 23
existence 85–7; after death 87–8

Falasifa 57, 82–3
Falsafa 1, 20, 21, 79, 109;
  contradictions 7; divine essence 18;
  history of 5–7
Fasl al-maqal (Ibn Rushd) 38, 71, 72,
  77–8, 77–9, 98, 128
Fechner, Gustav 51
fiqh see law
force, notion of 46
formalism 61, 63
Frederick II of Hohenstaufen 45, 127

Galen 46, 47, 49, 52
Gauthier, L. 80, 92
genetic analysis 54
geography 21
Gershon, Levi ben (Gersonides)
  (1288–1344) 125–6, 127
Gersonides *see* Gershon, Levi ben
Ghazalian temptation 8
Gilson, E. 92, 127
Giralda 20
God, attributes of 83–6; as cause 87;
  divine action 75; divine attributes
  72–3, 86, 118, 130; divine
  transcendence 73–4; freedom of 105;
  perfection of 75–6; proof of existence
  71–7; unicity of 82, 88; views of
  18–20; vision of 74–5
Gomez Nogales, S 4
grammar 94–5; Arabic 6; and logic 63
Granada 11
Grosseteste, Robert 45
Guide of the Perplexed (Ibn Maymun) 43,
  125

Ha-Levi, Juda 9, 122, 125
Ha-Levi of Seville, Moses ben Joseph
  124
Hanafi 65
Hanbali 65
Hayy 27, 81
Hayy Ibn Yaqzan (Ibn Tufayl) 28, 53
Hegel, George 99
helicoidal movement, hypothesis of
  44–5
henotheism 18
Hinduism 122
Hintata 16, 34

151

INDEX

Hippocrates 52
holy war/s 16, 17, 34–5, 113
human macrocosm, theory of 47
hylemorphism 104

Ibn Abi 'Usaybi'a 32, 47, 48
Ibn al-Abbar 31, 35, 48
Ibn al-Imam 7, 25
Ibn al-Mujahid 70, 109
Ibn al-Mu'tazz 60
Ibn al-Sic of Badajoz
  (444/1052–521/1127) 6, 63–4
Ibn Arabi 2, 118–20
Ibn Asakir 21
Ibn Atiya 11
Ibn Badis 121
Ibn Bajja (Avempace) (d 533/1138) 6,
  17, 26, 38, 42, 45–6, 48, 56, 93,
  101, 123; importance of 22; as
  influence on Ibn Rushd 8; and
  intellect 110; on logic and grammar
  63–4; theory of knowledge 7–8
Ibn Gabirol (c. 1020–1057) 5, 6
Ibn Ghanya 112
Ibn Hamdin, Grand Qadi of Cordoba
  (439/1047–508/1114) 11, 12–13
Ibn Harun de Trujillo, Abu Ja'far (al-
  Trujali) 32, 34, 48
Ibn Hasday, Yusuf 45
Ibn Hawt Allah, Abu Muhammed 70,
  117
Ibn Hazm 4, 6, 28, 66, 95; breadth of
  thought 8; as original thinker 5
Ibn Hussayn of Toledo 9
Ibn Junayd 118
Ibn Jurayyal 48
Ibn Mada, Qadi of North Africa
  (513/1119–592/1195) 94–5
Ibn Masarra of Cordoba
  (269/883–319/931) 4, 6, 22
Ibn Maymun (Maimonides)
  (1135–1204) 42–3, 64, 123–5
Ibn Quzman 59
Ibn Rushd, 3 periods of production
  36–8; characteristics of thought
  98–9; death 36; desire to organize
  knowledge 48; difficulty in placing
  99–100; disgraced 31, 34–6;
  education 32–3; funeral 120; as

influence 2, 67; as jurist 40;
  paradoxical 116–17, 131; as
  philosopher of nature 58; as Qadi of
  Seville and Cordoba 34, 118;
  standpoint of 30–1; strict outlook 92
Ibn Rushd wa falsafa tuhu (Farah Antun)
  120
Ibn Sab'in of Murcia 55, 61, 110, 117,
  128
Ibn Sina (Avicenna) (370/980–
  428/1037) 2, 5, 7, 26, 48, 60, 71,
  80, 85, 97–9, 105, 125, 127, 128;
  criticisms against 57–8; medical
  poem of 37
Ibn Taymiya 18
Ibn Tufayl (d 581/185/6) 24, 25–7, 53,
  71, 80, 110, 118, 119, 123; and
  astronomy 42; and Ibn
  Rushd 31–2
Ibn Tumart (c. 471–4/1078–
  81–524/1130) 11–12,
  13–14, 62–4, 81, 94, 105, 114;
  doctrine of 18; on existence 71–7,
  85–6; influence on Ibn Rushd 34; as
  leader of community 16; spiritual
  guides of 15–16; theology of 27; on
  time 84
Ibn Tumlus of Alcira 61, 117
Ibn Wafid, Abu-l-Mutarrif (c. 398/
  1007–467/1074) 48
Ibn Zuhr 40–1, 47
illumination 119; as illusion 26
illuminism 71
immorality, subjective 1
incarnation of order 54
India 121–2
individual 107; concept of 82
injustice 112
intellect, Agent 8, 102, 107, 108, 110;
  status of 8, 99–109; unity of 107–8;
  various 110
interpretation, allegorical 67
Isagogue (Porphyry) 92–3
Isidore of Seville, Saint 3, 4
Islam 16, 18, 122; beneficial influence
  4; culture 62; as practical system 13

Jahiz 63
Jews 5, 82, 122–7

INDEX

John of Padua 47
Jolivet, J. 102–4, 108
Judaism 18
judgement, themes of 88

Kairouan 5
Kairouan, conference at (1975) 121
Kalam 19, 35, 74, 78, 124; Ash'arite
83, 117
Kant 99
Kashf 'an manahij al-adilla 38, 71–7, 84
Kassem, M. 128
Khan, Sir Ahmad (1815–1898) 122
Kharijis 11, 65; doctrine 18, 20
Kitab al-Taysir (Abu Marwan) 47
knowledge, attainment of 110;
empirical 21; ontological foundations
93; pursuit of 22; two kinds of 72
Koran 15, 68
Kuzari (Ha-Levi) 122

Lahiji 120
Lamentatio Philosophiae (Lull) 129, 130
Lamentatio Raimundi (Lull) 130
language, Arabic 122; conceptual 106;
as misleading and inescapable
95
law (*fiqh*) 12–13, 19, 30, 69, 73;
Almohad view of 14–15; and
mysticism 9–10; proofs and solutions
65; religious 78; treatise on 37; two
types 95; works on 64–8
Leibniz 87
'Letters to the Community' (Ibn
Tumart) 16
Liber de causis (Proclus) 127
Liber natalis pueri Iesu (Lull) 129, 130
literalism, Zahiri 67
logic 61–4, 91; Aristotelian 6;
contribution to 92; Greek 6
Logos, doctrine of 81, 111
Lucan 3
Lucena, as place of exile 36
Lull, Ramon (1232–1316) 128–31

Maghreb 31; unrest in 35
Mahdi 16, 17, 19, 79, 82, 87, 102,
104, 110–11
Maimonides *see* Ibn Maymun

Majorca 117
Makhzan 16
Malik b. Wuhayb of Seville
(453/1060–524/1130) 6, 18, 25,
109
Malikis 17, 65, 66, 67, 69;
traditionalism 2
Malikism 12, 13
Maqasid al-Falasifa (al-Ghazali) 91,
128
Marahal of Prague 127
Marcilus of Padua 129
Marrakesh 33, 38, 43
Marti, Ramon (c. 1230–c. 1285)
128–31
Matta Ibn Yunus 62
Maymun (Marcus) 6
meaning, apparent and hidden 77
medicine, Aristotelian rules 50–1;
generalities 49; scholastic 53; study
of 46–54; three powers 52
Megarics 106, 107
metaphors 77, 93
metaphysics 104, 123
Metaphysics (Aristotle) 40, 91, 98, 102,
103, 126, 128
Meteorologies 39, 126
metonymy 93
Milky Way 43
miracles 76, 80–1
modernists 60
monotheism 18
Morata, N. 40
Multiple Averroes (Badawi) 59
muscles, study of 52–3
Muslims, in al-Andalus 3–5; current
thoughts 1–2; and science 21
Mustasfa (al-Ghazali) 35
Mutakallimun 92
Mutanabbi 60
Mu'tazilism 4
mutilation 12
mysticism, and *fiqh* 9–10

Narboni, Moses 126
necessary, criticism of 85–6
necessity, doctrine of 105, 106
neoplatonist/s 61, 90, 102, 104, 108,
123

INDEX

Nicomachean Ethics (Aristotle) 37, 90, 111, 126

observation, logic of 103
On Fevers (Galen) 46
On the Heavens 43, 45
On Theriac 37, 40
opposites 97–8
Organon (Aristotle) 60, 61, 92, 126

participation, doctrine of 107
Parva naturalia 40, 55, 126
Paravicin, 47
Peripatetics 95
philosophers 8, 109
Philosophia perennis 2
philosophy 70; as branch of culture 33; defence of 112; as exclusive 78; and *Falsafa* 57; first treatises 6; peripatetic 82; translations of 127
physico-medical theory 56
physics 123
Physics (Aristotle) 28, 40, 42, 45–6, 49, 56
pilgrimage 113
plants 22–3
Plato 38, 58, 66, 105, 106, 111, 113, 114
Poetics (Aristotle) 59, 60
poetry 59–60, 128
politico-religious movement 8, 18
Politics (Aristotle) 90, 111
Porphyry 92–3
Portuguese 34
Posterior Analytics (Aristotle) 38, 92
preformationism, theory of 52
Pricillianism 4
prime mover 58, 105
probability, judgement of 13
Proclus 127
Profession of faith (Ibn Tumart) 62, 72, 73, 81
promises and threats 12, 19
prophecy 76
Prophet, the 66
prophethood, theory of 80
Ptolemy 41–2, 45
Pugio Fidei (Marti) 128

Qays 25
Qusta b. Luqa 127
Questions of Logic 90, 95–6
Qur'an 70, 72, 76, 77, 80, 82

Ramakrishna 122
rationalism 64–5, 71, 72, 77, 80, 122, 125
reason/s 34, 119; chain 81; conception of 76; and faith 79; order of 71; rising by its own powers 27
reasoning 92–9
reasoning, by analogy 30–1; individual 13–14
Recemundo, Bishop 6, 122
Rectification of the Intellect (Abu-l-Salt) 61
reformist movement 121
Refutation (Ibn Hamdin) 11
Refutations of the Grammarians (Ibn Mada) 94
relatives 98
religion, for the masses 79; and science 120–1
Renaissance 127
Renan, Ernest 1, 34, 55, 59, 71, 79, 100, 108, 120, 128, 129
renunciation 9, 10
Republic (Plato) 38, 66, 111, 115, 126
resurrection 88
Revelation 17, 19, 31, 73, 74, 78, 80, 82, 83, 87, 88, 121; ambiguity in 75; analogy and opinion 13–14; problem of 5
Revival of the Religious Sciences (al-Ghazali) 9
rhetoric 93
Rhetoric (Aristotle) 55, 59, 61
Rodriguez Molero, F. 53

Sa'id of Toledo, quoted 3–4
Saragossa 5, 45
Sarton 91
Scholastics 127
science, development of 21–6; and religion 120–1
Scott, Michael 45, 127
semiology 49
Seneca 3
Sermo de Substantia Orbis 90

INDEX

Sermones contra errores Averrois (Lull) 130–1
Seville 34, 70, 71
Seville, library in 33
sexes, equality of 113–14
Shafi'i 13, 65, 66
Shari'a 112
Shi'ites 17, 65
Siger de Brabant 127
Silves 34
skies, discussion of 32, 33; study of 93
Socrates 105; declaration 117
Sophistical Refutations (Aristotle) 67, 93
soul 88, 99, 125; Aristotle's conception of 56; doctrine of 53
spheres, eccentric 42–3; nature of 84
Spinoza 72, 87
spiritual guides (Ibn Tumart) 15–16
Sufism 10
Suhrawardi 2
Summa contra gentiles 128
Sunni 57, 65, 66, 68
surgery 51
syllogisms 93; chains of 129; modally mixed 96
syncretism 11, 19, 25, 28, 58, 67, 110
synecdoche 93

Tafsir on the *Physics* 90
Tahafut al-Falasifa (al-Ghazali) 127
Tahafut al-tahafut 38, 71, 80–1, 82, 97, 104, 105, 126, 128
Taifa, period 69, 70
Talkhis, on *Republic* (Plato) 90; on *Treatise on Fevers* (Galen) 90
Tariq 21
Taysir (Ibn Zuhr) 40–1, 49
teaching, multi-displinary 70
telepathy 119
Tempier, Etienne 130
text, internal criticism 58–9; revealed 78
Theicrisi da halmodana vahaltadabir (Paravicini) 47

Themistius 96, 104, 108
theological apologetics (*kalam*) 9
theology 104–5
'Theology of Aristotle' 58
Theophrastus 95
thoughts, greatness of 110; integration of new forms 70; as passive 108
time 83, 84–5; consideration of 95–9
Toledo 48
Topics (Aristotle) 39, 93, 128
Tora 127
tradition 35, 67, 77, 109; prophetic 69
traditionalist 81
Treatise on plants (Ibn Bajja) 22–3
Treatise on the union of the Agent Intellect with man (Ibn Bajja) 8, 26, 126
truth 62, 77, 115; double 101, 130; gradated theory of 98

ultimate perfection 57
Ummayad, caliphate 29; dynasty 5
Ummayad, writers 60
understanding, two theories 56–7
universe 22; structure of 106
Usul al-Fiqh 66
Utbiya 30

Vajda, G. 124
Valencia 10
veil, wearing of 30
Vivekananda 122

Weber, Ernst 51
Well of Exile (Marahal of Prague) 127
William of Auvergne 45
wisdom, divine 75

Ya'qub al-Mansur, Sultan *see* Abu Yusuf Ya'qub

Zahiri 65, 67, 70
Zahirism 95